PENGUIN BOOKS

Lite Reading

FRANK DEFORD is a senior writer for *Sports Illustrated* and the author or coauthor of nine books, including the novel *Everybody's All-American.* In 1982 Mr. Deford was named Sportswriter of the Year by the National Association of Sportscasters and Sportswriters. He may occasionally be seen with his foot on the third rail, engaged in heated discussion about whether Lite Beer from Miller is less filling or tastes great.

Lite Reading

by Frank Deford

PENGUIN BOOKS

Penguin Books Ltd, Harmondsworth,
Middlesex, England
Penguin Books, 40 West 23rd Street,
New York, New York 10010, U.S.A.
Penguin Books Australia Ltd, Ringwood,
Victoria, Australia
Penguin Books Canada Limited, 2801 John Street,
Markham, Ontario, Canada L3R 1B4
Penguin Books (N.Z.) Ltd, 182–190 Wairau Road,
Auckland 10, New Zealand

First published in simultaneous hardcover and
paperback editions by Penguin Books 1984

LIBRARY OF CONGRESS CATALOGING IN PUBLICATION DATA
Deford, Frank.
  Lite reading.
  1. Advertising—Beer—United States.
2. Advertising campaigns—Case studies. 3. Miller
Brewing Company.   I. Title.
HF6161.B5D43   1984   659.1′966342   83-15131
ISBN 0 14 061.600 4
ISBN 0 14 00.6813 9 (pbk.)

Printed in the United States of America by
W. A. Krueger Co., New Berlin, Wisconsin
Text set in Linotron Cheltenham Book and
Linotron Memphis Medium Italic

The elements of the LITE beer labels, including "A Fine Pilsner Beer" and atten-
dant design and the word "LITE" in distinctive typographic style, are trade-
marks of Miller Brewing Company and are used by permission.

Photographs from television or other advertising material for LITE beer are
copyrighted by Miller Brewing Company and are used by permission.

Photographs on cover and pages 2, 29, 40, 50, and 65 (bottom) copyright ©
1982. Photographs on pages 6 and 7 copyright © 1977, 1978, 1980, 1981, 1982.
Photographs on pages 11, 14, 37, 42, 53, 61, 72, 77, and 94 copyright © 1981.
Photographs on pages 32 and 57 copyright © 1975. Photograph on page 33
copyright © 1983. Photographs on pages 34, 38, 48, 64, and 65 (top) copyright
© 1980. Photographs on pages 41 and 67 copyright © 1979. Photograph on page
44 copyright © 1976. Photographs on pages 45 and 91 copyright © 1978.

PENGUIN ALL-STARS:
Publisher: Alan C. Kellock
Editor: Cork Smith
Copy Chief: Ruth Randall
Production Manager: Eileen Schwartz
Production Supervisor: Annie DeVito
Design Director / Designer : Beth Tondreau
Designer/Illustrator: Mary A. Wirth
Junior Designer: Michèle Greiner

To that faithful 20 percent of beer drinkers
who drink 80 percent of the beer

Contents

The finest brew of wit, humor, and ice-cold facts

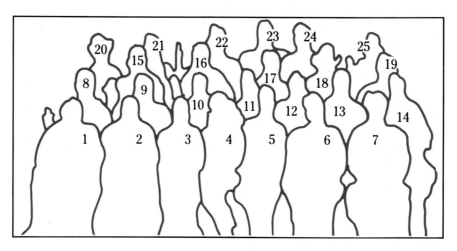

Here are the identities of the All-Stars shown on the cover and on the title page:

1. Bubba Smith
2. Jim Honochick
3. Frank Robinson
4. Lee Meredith
5. Billy Martin
6. Dick Williams
7. Red Auerbach
8. Steve Mizerak
9. Deacon Jones
10. Mickey Spillane
11. Rodney Dangerfield
12. Don Carter
13. Boom-Boom Geoffrion
14. Marv Throneberry
15. Dick Butkus
16. Boog Powell
17. Koichi Numazawa
18. Jim Shoulders
19. Matt Snell
20. Grits Gresham
21. Bob Uecker
22. Ray Nitschke
23. Ben Davidson
24. Tommy Heinsohn
25. John Madden

Lite Reading

Lite

A FINE PILSNER BEER

ALL STARS

Wanna Go Have a Few Beers?

There have been popular commercials before—commercials that set America's toes tapping, commercials that made us laugh, commercials that bored their way into our consciousness as surely as aspirins get into the bloodstream, commercials with jingles, commercials with Stan Freberg, commercials with money-back guarantees, commercials with sex, commercials with Mason Reese, commercials with cartoons, commercials with dogs, commercials with Arthur Godfrey. But none, absolutely none, has ever been so popular as the commercials for Lite Beer from Miller.

How popular are these commercials? They are so popular that a whole book has been done about them. You are reading it.

Have you ever met anybody who disliked the Lite campaign? Have you ever even met anybody who went to the bathroom when a Lite commercial came on the TV? "I would think that even the W.C.T.U. would at least have to appreciate our commercials," says Ben Davidson, ex-defensive lineman and prominent Lite All-Star, who has been included in the commercials since 1975, when he made his first one, in which he's shown knitting. But the campaign was already two years old when Davidson joined the team. The first Lite commercial was taped in July 1973, so the campaign has been going for more than a decade now, in itself something of a record in the transitory world of advertising.

By now, in fact, the Lite commercials have worked themselves into the public consciousness. They are part of us, part of the late-twentieth-century American existence, as sure as popcorn and stewardesses, weather forecasts, Elizabeth Taylor's marriages, french fries, green highway signs, Miss America, salad bars, joggers, Oscars and Osmonds, first loves, point spreads, Bob Hope, and Ronald Reagan. And, speaking of Bob Hope and Ronald Reagan, Hope said, not long ago: "President Reagan? He's not here. He's in Boston doing a Lite Beer commercial."

Lite Beer commercials are not passing fancies. They are not fads. They are not one-night stands. They'll be with us long after croissants and Perrier water have gone. Probably somewhere out there are people who snuggle up by the fire and recall "our Lite Beer commercial," as lovers once fell in love to "our song." Lite Beer commercials are with us. There are millions of American children whose ages are now in double digits who have never known intelligent life without them.

Plus, they work.

You see, some advertising campaigns are appreciated, even beloved, only they don't produce. Bottom line. They are just another pretty face. They sell themselves, but they don't sell the product. The classic of this genre was, in fact, a beer campaign—for a local New York brand known as Piel's. The Piel's commercials featured two cartoon brothers, Bert and Harry Piel, their voices those of Bob and Ray. Everybody loved Bert and Harry, but wouldn't buy the beer. Wouldn't touch the stuff. Past a certain point, a commercial is very much at the mercy of its product. The product and its advertising share a symbiotic relationship. I illustrate this very well myself.

Since I made my Lite commercial in 1981, people often ask me, Hey, level with me, you can tell me, do you really drink Lite Beer from Miller or did you just say that on the television because they paid you to? And the answer is, indeed I was remunerated for my efforts, but the truth is, I already drank Lite Beer because I loved the commercials so much that I tried the beer and loved it too.☆

When the Lite Beer commercials first got ahold of Lite Beer, it wasn't just a new brand of beer. It was a whole new concept in beer—a revolutionary beer, a diet beer, a lo-cal beer,☆☆ a . . . "Let's face it," says a prominent insider spokesman, a usually reliable source, "it was a fag beer." Yes, and by now, ten years later, Lite is not only the third-largest-selling beer in America,☆☆☆ but it has also spawned a complete new market of competitors. The Lite advertising didn't just sell Lite Beer—it created light beers.

In the process, it has brought a whole new level of fame to a bunch of retired athletes, like Ben Davidson. Ben, thirty-four other men, and one Doll currently comprise the Lite Beer All-Stars—"our two-legged Clydesdales,"☆☆☆☆ as they have been called at Backer & Spielvogel, the New York advertising agency that represents Miller Brewing. "The most popular team in the United States today isn't playing anybody. It's the Lite All-Stars," declares Al McGuire, former basketball coach, current TV commentator, longtime cultural student. John Griswold, the Backer & Spielvogel vice-president who is account director for Lite, says: "It's a cult now, the whole thing. The commercials are most like what *M*A*S*H* was, only we have new characters all the time."

Lite must use former athletes on its All-Star team, because active sports stars are prohibited from touting alcoholic products, and the popular television exposure has brought

☆ The reason for that is because it is less filling and tastes great.
☆☆ Lite has a third less calories than their regular beer.
☆☆☆ Budweiser and Miller High Life are at the top.
☆☆☆☆ An equine beast of burden, originally hailing from Clydesdale, Scot land, now playing professionally out of St. Louis, Missouri.

almost all of the All-Stars more recognition than they ever received as mere MVPs or world champions. Says Boog Powell☆: "You make one Lite commercial, it's like then everyone forgets you played ball for twenty years." Grits Gresham, the fisherman among the All-Stars, was once drinking wine in Rome when someone called to him: "Hey, shouldn't you be drinking a Lite Beer?" Every All-Star can relate comparable tales. Since I made my Lite commercial, I recognize a profound new appreciation for my work. People assume I surely must be a better writer inasmuch as I was a writer chosen to make a Lite Beer commercial.

Who am I to argue?

The Lite campaign has changed the way he-man types think about acting. There is an old French proverb, that an actress is more of a woman, but an actor is less of a man. "But acting is not perceived as sissy anymore," says Bob Giraldi, who has directed more Lite commercials than anyone. "Not any longer. Any athlete who still thinks acting is sissy is a real jerk." Says All-Star Billy Martin: "I wouldn't have done this thirty years ago."

Backer & Spielvogel have won all sorts of industry awards for creativity with Lite. Regularly, a company called Video Storyboard Tests Incorporated conducts thousands of interviews to determine the Hit Parade of favorite commercials, and time after time Lite finishes on top. In 1982 it won resoundingly over Coke, with Federal Express, McDonald's, and Pepsi rounding out the top five. The popularity of the Lite commercials is all the more impressive because usually the ads people favor most feature rosy-cheeked kids singing and smiling and generally ingratiating themselves. Eight of the top twenty-five favorite commercials last year were loaded with kids.

Lite commercials are simply different. In the world of video art, they are Dutch miniatures. Especially in their own

☆ As in: "Hey, you're Boog Powell!"

category, they break the mold. Almost all beverage commercials seem to consist of a great deal of singing and shouting. Whether it is El Exigente picking the coffee beans, or the world getting its head on straight with Coke, or telephone workers guzzling Miller High Life after a hard day up with the wires—coffee, soda pop, beer, whatever—there's a great deal of singing, and everybody is so nice you hate their candied guts. (The exception is decaffeinated coffee commercials, where everybody is miserable, edgy, and all over everybody else's case.)

But Lite commercials feature only a modicum of rhythmic treacle. Quick: how many of the eighty-one Lite commercials that have appeared on the air (as of this writing) have any music in them? Any music at all, even just one note.

Well, I'm going to give you the answer. When you turn the page you will find the Official Lite Beer from Miller Test. All of the answers appear somewhere in the pages of this volume, but if you're lazy or don't test well, the certified list of answers appears on page 96.

You will, however, get one free answer, just like the bonus "X" in the middle of the Bingo game. So, the answer to the first question—how many Lite commercials have music in them?—is six.

Now, you can look at the pictures, read the words, read the short words, or skip everything and jump directly to the test answers. Take your time, read the questions carefully, and bear down with a sharp, stubby pencil. There will be no talking once the test starts. If you want to go to the bathroom, raise your hand. If you want a beer, make a noise something like a bottle cap popping.

There are three parts. Part One is multiple choice, so you can guess your way through that. Part Two is for experts who think they know all the answers. Part Three is a bonus question.

Remember, every question is answered *somewhere* in this book.

THE **GRAND** AND **GLORIOUS**

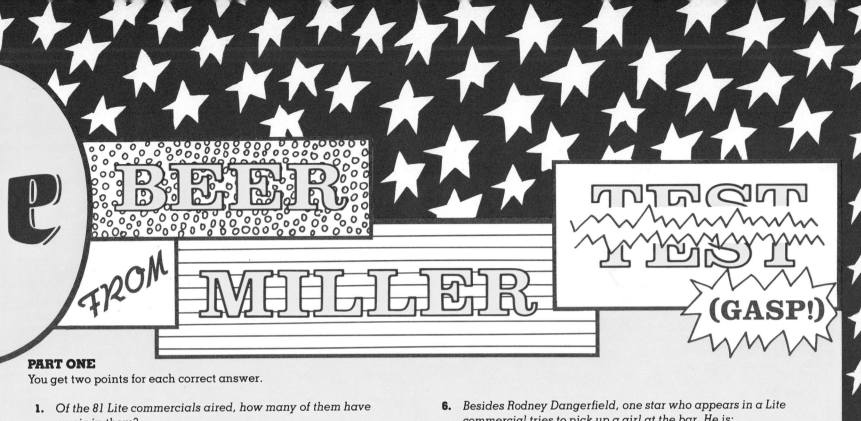

BEER FROM MILLER TEST TEST (GASP!)

PART ONE

You get two points for each correct answer.

1. Of the 81 Lite commercials aired, how many of them have music in them?
(a) none   b) six   c) 16   d) 22

2. Of the 36 present All-Stars, who is the oldest?
a) Red Auerbach   b) Mickey Spillane
c) Jim Honochick   d) Marv Throneberry

3. Who is the youngest?
a) Lee Meredith   b) Rodney Marsh   c) Steve Mizerak
d) Carlos Palomino

4. In Lite Beer commercial No. 20, two famous horses appear. They are:
a) Affirmed and Alydar   b) Secretariat and Riva Ridge
c) Foolish Pleasure and Honest Pleasure
d) Genuine Risk and Seattle Slew

5. Members of which team appear most in Lite commercials?
a) Yankees   b) Packers   c) Orioles   d) Celtics

6. Besides Rodney Dangerfield, one star who appears in a Lite commercial tries to pick up a girl at the bar. He is:
a) Marv Throneberry   b) Wilt Chamberlain
c) Paul Hornung   d) George Steinbrenner

7. Circle all the foreign languages that are spoken in Lite commercials:
a) Spanish   b) French   c) Polish
d) Bubbatalk   e) Japanese

8. Who is the only star in a commercial to sign his autograph?
a) Marv Throneberry   b) Bob Uecker
c) Rodney Dangerfield   d) Jerry Parent

9. Suddenly, in 1976–77, one item of clothing became fashionable for guys in Lite commercials. It was:
a) a fedora   b) an ascot
c) a leather jacket   d) a T-shirt

10. What does it say on lumberjack Brian Anderson's suspenders?
a) L. L. Bean   b) 6–5/8   c) Timber   d) Pull

11. Who gets the Doll besides Mickey Spillane?
a) Paul Hornung   b) Steve Mizerak
c) Ben Davidson   d) the Van Arsdale twins

12. Who is the only Lite drinker to appear in a commercial shot in a locker room?
a) Whitey Ford   b) Sam Jones
c) Deacon Jones   d) Dave DeBusschere

13. Who is the only Lite drinker to appear in a commercial shot on a football field?
a) Paul Hornung   b) Ernie Stautner
c) Buck Buchanan   d) Rosie Grier

14. Lite commercial No. 3 stars the first coach (or manager) ever to appear for Lite. He is:
a) Whitey Herzog   b) Whitey Ford
c) Tommy Heinsohn   d) Ernie Stautner

15. The first words out of Matt Snell's mouth in the first Lite Beer from Miller commercial are:
a) "You know, Lite Beer from Miller has everything you always wanted in a beer . . . and less."
b) "Listen, I'm a big guy with a big thirst."
c) "When you're not so light yourself, you need a Lite beer."
d) "New Lite Beer is a super beer, and you'd have to tackle me to keep me from one."

16. What part of Lee Meredith's anatomy caused problems during the shooting of her first Lite commercial?
a) legs   b) hair   c) breasts   d) hands

17. Who is the first All-Star to keep his hat on in a bar during the commercial?
a) Mickey Spillane   b) Grits Gresham
c) Jim Shoulders   d) Billy Martin

18. Which of the commercials features the largest number of famous Lite drinkers?
a) tug-o'-war   b) the anniversary photograph
c) softball   d) bowling

19. Of all the current All-Stars, only one has ever had his name mentioned in a Lite commercial that he did not appear in. He is:
a) Billy Martin   b) Boog Powell
c) Bubba Smith   d) Lee Meredith

20. In all 81 Lite commercials, only once does a star talk on the phone. He is:
a) Mike Roberts   b) James Drury
c) Nick Buoniconti   d) George Steinbrenner

21. Dick Butkus was a former football player, but in Lite ads he appears as a participant in these other sports (circle all the correct answers if more than one):
a) hiking   b) bowling   c) swimming   d) golf
e) mountain climbing   f) tennis   g) dog training

Scoring two points for each correct answer, there is a possible 50 points you could have scored so far.

PART TWO
Here we separate the men from the boys, the sheep from the goats, the wheat from the chaff, the Lites from the imitations. One point for each correct answer.

1. All right, who are all the Orioles who have appeared as famous Lite drinkers? There are seven. Three of them are Frank Robinson, Brooks Robinson, and Boog Powell. (Everybody knows that so you certainly don't get any credit for them.) Name the other four.

2. *Lite commercials use all these fantastic athletes, but in only one do we see any trophies. Which All-Star is featured in that commercial?*

3. *Which commercial is shown over with only one word changed? You must name the celebrity who utters the word and state what the word is.*

4. *Two prominent baseball announcers have appeared in Lite commercials—one in the past, one currently—in important roles, but were never made All-Stars. They are:*

5. *Name the two All-Stars who participated in the first Less Filling/Tastes Great argument.*

6. *Name the three All-Stars who defected to Natural Light commercials.*

7. *In only one of the 81 commercials aired is the expression "Everything you always wanted in a beer . . . and less" not included. Name it.*

8. *Sure, all those Celtics have played for Auerbach. What other current All-Star has had another current All-Star as his coach?*

9. *Sure, Steinbrenner fired Martin. But what current All-Star fired another current All-Star?*

10. *What's the difference between Frank and Brooks Robinson?*

11. *The second time Jim Honochick says, "Hey, you're Boog Powell," it is really———?*

12. *What does "Dlaczego Amerykaminowi zabraklo lodu?" mean, and who says it?*

13. *We know two famous horses appear in one Lite commercial. In how many other commercials are animals included? What kinds of animals?*

14. *What All-Star says he is only a "pussy cat"?*

15. *What All-Star quotes Big Daddy Lipscomb and Humphrey Bogart in two different commercials?*

16. *Name the only All-Star who has died.*

17. *What Miller Lite All-Star first came to fame on a Budweiser team?*

18. *Name all the athletes mentioned in Lite commercials who have never appeared in one. (Hint: they're all baseball players.)*

19. *In three Lite commercials there is talking in unison by two people. What commercials feature pairs talking?*

20. *Who is the only All-Star to appear in a Lite commercial (two, in fact) in his regular big-league uniform?*

21. *In one Lite commercial, two of the All-Stars are not identified. They also don't speak. Who are they? And what are they doing?*

Scoring one point per correct answer, you can score a possible 46 points in this section.

PART THREE

A perfect score would be 96. But if you want to shoot for 100, try this one for 4 points:

What do you think, is Lite Beer from Miller less filling or do you prefer it because it tastes great?

Gimme a Lite

*I*t is nothing new to use athletes to advertise a product, although initially the most common procedure was managed without the players' acquiescence. That is, cigarette companies once inserted picture cards of major-league baseball players into their packs without permission. (Nowadays, players receive a small recompense when their pictures are put in bubble-gum packages.) In fact, the most valuable baseball card of all is a Honus Wagner, because the Flying Dutchman abstained from tobacco, and therefore forced a cigarette company to withdraw his likeness from their collection.

But the employment of athletes as product endorsers grew. It is recorded in history that in 1919, when Babe Ruth learned that he had been sold from the Red Sox to the Yankees, his first reaction was to bemoan the fact that this would separate him from a Boston cigarmaker whose product he favored. Subsequently athletes began to stumble through tributes on the radio, mouthing such encomiums as, "It tastes good, and it's good for you, too." Or they appeared in print, exhibiting their T-zones for Camel cigarettes. Mostly, though, the endorsement arena was left to bona fide entertainers—actors and actresses whose visages were instantly recognizable from the silver screen.

Television changed everything. Until TV, athletes were seldom identifiable to the world at large, with the exception, perhaps, of the first superstars: men like Babe Ruth or Jack

Dempsey, Joe Louis, maybe a handful of others. No golfer or tennis player, not to mention anyone so esoteric as a basketball or hockey star, would have been recognized away from the playing fields. Oh, possibly by Dad or Junior, if they were big fans; certainly never by Mom or Sis.

This began to change around 1960. A variety of factors were at play. First of all, professional sports were growing in prominence, at the expense of amateur games. The big stars were willing and quite capable of plugging for pay. Moreover, with television, the jock—a word that began to enjoy respectable usage at about that time—began to force his way into the living room. It even became commonplace for former athletes, who, in the past, had gone back to the hardware store, or to selling insurance, or possibly to gladhanding at some saloon or beefsteak bistro, to move in front of the cameras as commentators or analysts—"color men," as they began to be called. To see an athlete, active or retired, in mufti became an everyday experience.

Some jocks, it was discovered, could talk.

At the same time, Hollywood was being splintered, losing much of its allure and glamour. Besides, anytime a company uses an actor to tout its product, it begs the question of anyone watching: Is this guy still acting, is this just another role?

Athletes, on the other hand, were still perceived as common folk.They were engaged in physical exercise, which was becoming chic, and they were generally assumed to be wholesome and honest, just like you or me, only with a tad more coordination. Certainly, they were not paid the gargantuan amounts of money that actors received, and they knew not from agents. This kept their All-American Boy status intact, while making them all the more attractive to sponsors. Steve Arnold, one of the pioneers in the field of sports agentry, recalls, when he was still working for an advertising agency in 1964, being dispatched to see if a leading NFL quarterback would be interested in making a commercial.

Arnold was prepared to pay several thousand dollars for the fellow's services, but, idly, he inquired of the quarterback what he thought would be a fair price. "Would $100 an hour be too much?" the poor jock asked.

The value of the athlete as pitchman should, perhaps, have been more obvious all along. Jantzen had used a collection of clean-cut pros to pose for what it called the Jantzen International Sports Club, and that campaign ran, with great success, for almost fifteen years, before it was junked in the mid-sixties when a new ad agency took over the account. "I knew it had to be working—even after I retired from playing—because of the recognition I kept getting," Bob Cousy says. And those are, of course, precisely the words echoed by the Lite All-Stars today.

Cousy is unique, spanning two sports advertising generations. He is a current member of the Lite All-Stars, more than a quarter century after he and Frank Gifford started off as the two charter Jantzen Sports Clubbers. Soon, other heroes were piped aboard, the likes of Don Meredith, Paul Hornung,☆ and Terry Baker from football, Dave Marr and Ken Venturi from golf, Bobby Hull of hockey, Jerry West of basketball. It was a congenial, homogeneous crowd, absolutely lily-white until late in the day, when Timmy Brown, an NFL running back, was added to the roster.

The Sports Clubbers never did any television commercials, though. Instead, once a year they would assemble at some attractive location—most often the Royal Hawaiian Hotel on Waikiki—and go through a day or two of photographic modeling sessions, for pictures that would be used in Jantzen catalogs or popular magazines. The Clubbers had to change into literally hundreds of outfits. They would get photographed on the lawn or the beach, then dash inside the hotel to a distant men's room, change, and run back out again. Finally, exhausted by this routine, Cousy and Gifford

☆ Later a Lite All-Star.

discovered a well-placed potted palm in the lobby. They would run in, duck behind it, and there, in the lobby of the Royal Hawaiian Hotel, while visiting matrons strolled about, America's heroes would take off their clothes, pull a new pair of Jantzen trunks over their jockstraps, and run back outside again.

The Jantzen International Sports Club may not have been very sophisticated, but its demise must be lamented, for it was obviously a gimmick of inspired genius, serving as the forefather for the two most disparate and successful sports advertising campaigns of the present day. On the one hand, the Jantzen beefcake presaged Jim Palmer's unveiling in Jockey briefs. On the other, it showed how a group of athletes, a team of stars, could be united behind a product, as has been the case with Lite.

But first it was at the local level where athletes were able to show themselves most effectively as pitchmen. It is common for sports stars to bemoan the fact that they are not playing in New York or Los Angeles, media/entertainment/advertising centers where they could obtain the most endorsement income, but, in fact, this is something of a myth, except perhaps where the very biggest stars are concerned. The truth is that pro athletes can pick up lucrative endorsement work in the relatively smaller major-league cities, where they have much less competition. For example, in Cincinnati, except perhaps for a disc jockey or TV weatherman, who else would the local Toyota dealer get to pitch his product but some Red or Bengal player? In the major markets, athletes face competition from a more compelling lot of celebrities.

So it was in the sixties that, out in the boondocks, athletes began to share the endorsement trade. Perhaps the most famous local spot was aired in the San Francisco Bay area, for a product known as Saxon Apple Juice. The ad agency signed up Juan Marichal, the Giants' star pitcher, as the Saxon spokesman. Marichal's line on the radio commercials was: "Saxon Apple Juice will make you feel strong." Only with his Dominican accent, it came out sounding like this: "Sex and apple juice will make you feel strong."

Soon the major ad agencies in New York were beginning to turn regularly toward athletes. Late in the 1960s, O. J. Simpson signed a quarter-of-a-million-dollar contract with Chevrolet, a deal that exploded across all the barriers. First of all, it was at that time almost certainly the largest endorsement amount ever given to any athlete, but beyond that, Simpson was a black athlete, laboring in the vineyards of Buffalo, New York. About the same time, Gale Sayers and Cazzie Russell were chosen to endorse Ideal Toys; Jim Brown, Elgin Baylor, and

Oscar Robertson were among the athletes selected to speak up for Desenex; and Matt Snell was one of the New York Jets used in a commercial for Score hair dressing.

Nothing, however, generated so much attention as a $10,000 deal another New York Jet signed. For that amount, Broadway Joe Namath agreed to shave off his controversial Fu Manchu mustache with a Schick electric razor.☆ The furor surrounding this episode was such that Namath's shave may yet remain the most famous single commercial of all time. Schick and its ad agency deemed it so special that the commercial was shown only one time apiece on each of the three networks. It was an *event*.

By this time athletes were enjoying so much success endorsing products that the Fellowship of Christian Athletes began to utilize similar methods to reach its potential constituency. The F.C.A. was especially put out that Namath, who was considered a sybarite in some circles, was being presented in prime time by commercial America, and so Christian heroes were urged to use Madison Avenue wiles to attract youthful parishioners.

Meanwhile, back in New York, one advertising executive not only began to specialize in employing athletes in commercials, but to slot them in most original ways. His name was George Lois, and he had attended Pratt Institute in New York City on half a basketball scholarship. He remained an unregenerate sports nut who knew not only the names of players, but also their idiosyncrasies.

"The ad must transcend the fact that you're using an athlete," he said. "You don't just say, Hey, let's get a ballplayer for this. There must be a legitimate reason. You use a particular athlete only when it is apt to do so, or, on the other side of the coin, in never-never land, when it is so ridiculous to use an athlete that it becomes a good bit for everybody."

So it was that Lois, for his famous Odd Couple campaign for Braniff Airlines, put Sonny Liston in the seat next to Andy Warhol, listening to Warhol talk about art; had Whitey Ford sit next to Salvador Dali and tell him a few of the niceties of pitching; and had Mickey Spillane sit next to another published author, someone Spillane remembers only as "this little old lady in a tricornered hat."☆☆ For a brokerage house, Edwards & Hanly, Lois hired on Mickey Mantle, who said, "When I first came up to the big leagues, I was a grinnin', shufflin', head-duckin' country boy. Well, I'm still a country boy, but I know a man down at Edwards & Hanly. I'm learnin'. I'm learnin'." Joe Louis, whose financial plight had been well publicized, was even more to the point.

☆ Some years before, the Yankee shortstop Tony Kubek had agreed to let his crew cut go long so he could get $3000 for saying Vitalis kept his hair "neat all day without grease . . ."
☆☆ It was the poet Marianne Moore.

"Edwards & Hanly, where were you when I needed you?" he asked plaintively.

Other agencies began to see the value of using athletes in situations where their special personae could be applied most effectively. Volkswagen got Wilt Chamberlain to show how roomy the Bug was. A plethora of NFL right guards was assembled in order to tout the deodorant of the same name. Long before Jim Palmer took to displaying his body, he was hired to push pancakes, inasmuch as it had been revealed that he had eaten pancakes before beating Sandy Koufax for his first World Series victory. Mail Pouch chewing tobacco even hired a pitcher, Lew Burdette, to praise the properties of that brand. "Bring back the spitter," Burdette petitioned.

With these types of commercials, the art was moving into a new stage, which relied greatly on humor—especially the kind edged with self-deprecation. In fact, the Lite commercials would never reach the heights until they began to lean on this formula. Lois used it more and more all the time. For a hot cereal named Maypo, he signed on a number of he-man athletes—Mantle (Lois was crazy about the Mick), Chamberlain, Ray Nitschke of the Packers—to tear up and bawl, "I want my Maypo, I want my Maypo." Cereal sales increased 10 percent, but students of commercials might have also paid attention to the identity factor—what Bob Cousy had noticed a few years before, when he kept being recognized for Jantzen long after he had disappeared from the basketball court.

The Maypo commercials were aired only on kiddie programs, so most adults had no idea they even existed. After Don Meredith made one, his Dallas Cowboy teammates were utterly mystified when young fans gathered about Meredith and then suddenly started whining and crying, imitating his Maypo bit.

Something else was starting. In an odd way, fans were beginning to identify with their heroes more for how they were portrayed in commercials than for what they accomplished on the playing field—which had gotten them the commercials in the first place. The same sort of bizarre reasoning began to be exerted by the ad agencies in determining which athletes were selected for commercials. A star who had made one commercial was more likely to be chosen for another with another product. Why? He's made a commercial, hasn't he? Ergo, he's well known. Art follows art.

Remember Matt Snell, the black New York Jet chosen to sing in the Score commercial? Sure you do. Well, Snell was then selected for an Off-Track Betting print advertisement, and his smiling face went up on buses and subways all over New York City.

I'll Have Another

In 1969, the Philip Morris tobacco company, seeking to diversify its operations, closed out a deal to buy Miller Brewing for $227,000,000. It turned out to be one of the outstanding acquisitions of this corporate era, but at the time it drew little attention. Miller, led by its flagship brand, High Life, owned only a 4.2 percent share of the national market,☆ standing in seventh place, far behind Anheuser-Busch, which boasted an 18.2 percent share. High Life had sort of a pantywaist, country-club im-

age; for years its precious symbol had been that of a pretty girl sitting on a new moon. High Life wasn't even better than Number Three in its own hometown, Milwaukee. There Pabst Blue Ribbon ranked just ahead of Miller, and Schlitz ruled them both. Schlitz was a real man's beer, a dark bottle with a dark label, a tough beer, The Beer That Made Milwaukee Famous, the only genuine challenger to Budweiser, all alone down there in St. Louis.

While Bud was the country's leading beer, brewing had remained, until quite recently, a predominantly local endeavor. As late as the turn of the century there were two thousand different breweries in America; when Prohibition

☆ Some 122,000,000 barrels were sold annually in the U.S. at that time. Since there are 436 bottles of beer to a barrel, that's a lot of suds.

was repealed in 1933, there remained seven hundred and fifty breweries ready to start up again and begin turning out beers. Today there are less than fifty different breweries. Most beer drinkers were—and are—notoriously brand-loyal, and it was even more a point of pride to stick with your beer if it was of local origin. Most people would no more drink a national brand of beer than they would drink milk that had been bottled thousands of miles away.

As good an example of this as any is the city of Baltimore, where I grew up and first tasted a cold beer. All the formative beers I remember in Baltimore were local: Gunther and Arrow, American and the Nationals—National Bohemian and its highfalutin sidekick, National Premium. I suppose there were some people who drank "imports" from places like Milwaukee and St. Louis, but I sure didn't know such people. The local beers so ruled the territory that National actually ended up with a major-league team named after it. When National started bringing us☆ the Washington Senators' games from down the road, it changed the team name to "the Nationals" for a while. The team's slogan was: "I'm nuts about the Nats," which may account for the fact most people kept on calling them the Senators anyway.

The long tradition of drinking local beer was in keeping with the old German custom, where almost every neighborhood—let alone every town—had its own brewery. ☆☆ A century ago, in Bavaria alone there were more than six thousand breweries. Germany, of course, is still renowned as the premier beer country in the world, and bier☆☆☆ is nearly treated as a natural resource. West German law still prohib-

its anything but the four basic ingredients to be used in any beer brewed within its borders. These standard elements are barley malt—which is often referred to as the "soul" of the beer—water, yeast, and hops.

Beer's origins can be traced far from the Rhineland, however. There is evidence that a beer-type drink was available in China as early as the twenty-third century B.C., and in Egypt, somewhat later, the legend grew that brewing had been introduced to those precincts by none other than Isis, the goddess of life.

In America, the finer breweries did not really begin to develop until the mid-nineteenth century, when the heaviest German immigration began, the newcomers bringing with them the lighter beers preferred along the Rhine to compete with the darker, stronger ale, with its predominantly British antecedents. (Originally, the distinction between ale and beer was carefully defined, the latter containing less alcohol and more hops, but nowadays it tends to be only a matter of the different yeasts employed.) But make no mistake: beer was always prominent in the New World. Beer, rum, and cider were the three favorite spirits, right from the first.

Whereas we are encouraged to think of the Pilgrims as a pious, abstemious lot, the fact is that the *Mayflower* sat low in the water when it sailed, weighted down with forty monstrous casks of ale. Furthermore, had there been somewhat

---

☆ Beer companies always say that they "bring you" a team they sponsor.

☆☆ Baltimore was a good German city then, too. In backyards there were little areas set aside, known as beer gardens. Fooling no one, we call beer gardens "patios" today. Oh, well.

☆☆☆ Directly from the Latin *bibere*, to drink.

more spirits aboard, the whole early course of American history would have changed, and there would be no Thanksgiving Day parades on television. It seems that the wayfarers preferred a more benign landing spot than Plymouth Rock; in fact, they had in mind going all the way down the coast to Virginia, and would have, but for the fact that "we could not now take time for further search or consideration, our victuals being much spent, especially our beer."

But, not to worry. As early as 1623 the Dutch had a brewery going on these shores, right in Manhattan, only a few miles from where most Lite Beer from Miller commercials are written and taped. Even more prescient was the Virginia Assembly, which encouraged newcomers to be sure to bring large supplies of malt to the New World in order that they might "continue to brew and drink beer until their bodies were hardened to the drinking water" in America. And of course, as every schoolchild knows, this historical fact set the stage for Lite Beer commercial No. 51, starring former welterweight champion Carlos Palomino, wherein he advises some Hispanic friends: "When you come to America, drink Lite Beer . . . but don't drink the water."

William Penn himself founded a brewery near Philly, not far from where Jim Honochick, the former umpire and most venerable Lite All-Star, hails from. At Mount Vernon, down the river from where Deacon Jones once anchored the Redskin defense, George Washington boasted of his own brewery, one that produced a very honored product in those parts. It was upon the floor of a Baltimore brewery that a Mrs. Pickersgill and her daughter sewed the American flag that was to fly over Fort McHenry, where its very broad stripes and bright stars inspired "The Star Spangled Banner."

And quick, what are the last two words of our National Anthem?

Answer: Play ball.

Surely, of all sports, baseball has been most closely associated with beer. Much of this no doubt has to do with the fact that more beer is consumed in the hot days of summer, when baseball is played. (We think of football first as a sport men bring flasks to, to nip at and keep their innards warm.) A century ago, the Cincinnati Reds, the first professional baseball team in the world, dropped out of the National League and remained out for several seasons because of a foolish local ordinance that prohibited beer being sold in the ballpark. Last year, 1983, when the Cardinals happened to open their season on a special Election Day, everyone was horrified to discover that the city banned the sale of alcoholic beverages while the polls were open and democracy was being renewed. But in this instance, in an illustration of how far civilization has marched in a hundred years on its way from Cincinnati to St. Louis, wiser heads prevailed, the laws were tinkered with, and beer was sold at Busch Stadium.

Growing up in Baltimore, we even had an expression, "Ain't the beer cold!?!," which meant terrific, fantastic, wow—or totally awesome, if you are a Valley Girl. As far as I know, I first heard this exclamation from Chuck Thompson, who was—and still is, bless his heart—the play-by-play announcer for the Orioles. Chuck's beer was National Bohemian, which, of course, brought us the Orioles. It remains although so many other local brands have disappeared. Even Ballantine is gone from New York—Ballantine, which used to bring us the Yankees and "Ballantine Blasts," which were home runs hit by Yankees and described by Mel Allen.

Oh, a few local beers hang on—Iron City in Pittsburgh, say, or Hudepohl in Cincy—but more and more the large national breweries have been biting into the local markets. In a more sophisticated commercial universe, the nationals, led by the Anheuser-Busch juggernaut, possessed certain marketing advantages that could overcome even local pride. Perhaps the nationals gained a tremendous edge in advertising as sports became, just like beers, more national in character.

The president of another major brewery, the fourth largest in the country, sums up the situation very neatly: "If you're not advertising nationally on sporting events, then you're not reaching beer-drinking men very efficiently."

The simple connection between beer and sports is that sports fans tend to be men and men tend to drink the most beer. Research indicates that about 20 percent of beer drinkers consume about 80 percent of the beer, and most of this 20 percent is made up of males who have reached the legal age, but haven't crossed hopelessly into middle age—twenty-one to forty, that general crowd. Every major beer seeks this constituency.

Essentially, it becomes a vicious circle. A beer that wishes to survive must reach that large target center in order to do so. But those drinkers are not dumb, not sheep. And, as we shall see from the woeful Schlitz experience, a bad beer cannot sell, no matter how good the marketing and advertising.

Of course, a small percentage of drinkers continue to demand something unusual. Three percent of the United States market is constituted of foreign beer sales, and another two and a half percent of sales comes from some domestic brands that are still made in small breweries. Perhaps the most famous of these is Anchor Steam, of San Francisco. The major breweries refer to Anchor Steam and its ilk as "boutique breweries."

While the trend to centralization among beer drinkers was accelerating, there was one bit of diversionary action. As sure as athletes were becoming more fashionable in America, Americans were also becoming more health-conscious. People were growing more careful about how much they weighed. No-cal! Carbohydrates and cholesterol (whatever they may be) were discovered. Implicit in the expression "beer belly" is the suggestion that he who drinks a lot of beer is inclined to put on weight, develop an unattractive gut, and maybe die early. The trend toward "light" alcoholic beverages was under way—clear vodka instead of hard whiskey, or even sissy wine, chosen as a drink away from the communion rail.

Americans do put away a lot of beer—more than 30 billion dollars' worth annually, which comes out to twenty-five gallons a year per adult—but there is obviously room for improvement, inasmuch as we stand a measly twelfth in per capita consumption around the world. Some people in the business began to muse that the beer market might be expanded in keeping with the times. A beer that could be touted as being in tune with slimness and style might have a future, sort of like menthol cigarettes or Nehru suits. A fine old brewery in Chicago named Meister Brau brought out such a brand, naming it Meister Brau Lite. In New York Rheingold created a brand named Gablinger's and launched this new low-calorie beer with a great deal of fanfare.

Matt Snell was still playing for the New York Jets at that time, and was doing some promotional work for Rheingold. The brewery sent him some of the new stuff and asked him to give Gablinger's a try. He was a big stocky guy, and maybe a lo-cal beer would be just right for him. Snell remembers Gablinger's very well. "It tasted like frozen ice water," he says.

These Three
Are on Me

I'll Get These Four

Marty Blackman was one of the first lawyers to start representing sports clients. An early catch of his was Bubba Smith, who was the first player drafted in 1967 into the National Football League. Smith, who came from Beaumont, Texas, later explained to Blackman why he had not been especially friendly when Blackman had first started pitching him. "I was told to be careful of white men, " Bubba said. Blackman is white. "I was told to be careful of people from New York." Blackman is from New York. "I was told to be careful of fast-talking guys." Blackman is fast-talking. "I was told to be careful of Jews." Blackman is . . .you get the picture. "I was told to be careful of lawyers."

Despite these drawbacks, Blackman had considerable success representing players, but he perceived an even greater opportunity if he worked another part of the forest. There were more and more guys willing to represent athletes, but when it came to endorsements, the advertising agencies had little expertise. There were very few admen like George Lois, able to marry the right athlete to the right spot. "Even now," Blackman says, "four-fifths of the people involved in casting for TV are women. And certainly at that time, back in the sixties, few of those women were fans who knew anything about sports."

As a consequence, when someone at the agency said, "Get me a jock," the women casting experts had no real knowledge of where to go. In most cases they just went to the most familiar name, the one they'd heard at lunch or at Saturday's cocktail party. More often than not, the name turned out to be the current star of a local New York team. From Madison Avenue, no sweat was believed to exist in America except at Yankee and Shea Stadiums. It is a fact that Y. A. Tittle, the Giants quarterback, was once approached about appearing in a hair tonic commercial—and, of course, Tittle's trademark was his shining pate. Had been for years, no less than Yul Brynner's; or Steve Mizerak's cue ball. A few years later Brooks Robinson was actually signed to appear in a commercial for Vitalis, and not a single person involved in the endeavor realized that Robinson was himself prematurely balding until he showed up before the cameras with his very high forehead.

They tried to shoot around it.

Blackman began making the rounds of the agencies, identifying himself as a knowledgeable sports agent who could steer an ad firm to the right jock. He carved out some work for his clients, too, but he really made his mark when an agency doing an after-shave lotion commercial came to him. They had a certain player already in mind, but they wanted to know if Blackman concurred that it would be a wise choice. Blackman didn't know the player in question, so he said he'd make a few calls. Surprisingly, he began to receive some strangely negative insinuations. Nobody would tell Blackman anything outright, but the reports were all guarded. Finally, Blackman urged the after-shave people to lay off this guy. He didn't know why, but "there's something out there." Reluctantly, the after-shave agency turned to another athlete. Their original choice kept playing and starring. The agency was not happy with Marty Blackman and his instincts.

It was a few months later that the original player in question was picked up on well-publicized morals charges.

Thereafter, helped by the grateful after-shave company,

the word began to circulate around Madison Avenue that Marty Blackman was the right guy to contact for good, clean (and possibly articulate) jocks. "To this day," Blackman says, "the All-Stars must be two things above all. First, they must present the image that they're a guy you want to have a beer with. And second, they must be socially clean." ☆

And so it was, early in 1973, that Blackman got a call from the McCann-Erickson agency, which was looking for some recognizable big, manly types, beer guys. Athletes could certainly be included in this group, although because of the regulations prohibiting active athletes from endorsing alcoholic beverages, they would have to be retired players.

McCann-Erickson's client, Miller Brewing, was thinking about doing something with Meister Brau Lite. There were approximately two things that went through most people's minds at McCann-Erickson. One was Gablinger's, Matt Snell's "frozen ice water." Never mind that most people, like Snell, had found that product execrable. The advertising campaign for Gablinger's was still writ large in the annals of Madison Avenue disasters.

The Gablinger's campaign had spoken of the low-calorie properties of the beer and of the values of slimness and moderation. Figure it out: the main reason why those 20 percent of beer drinkers consume 80 percent of all beer sold is precisely because they never stop with a singleton. Schaefer, an Eastern beer, has always spoken best to that, with its classic jingle: "Schaefer is the one beer to have when you're having more than one." By contrast, Gablinger's advertising turned off the prime beer buyers because not only did it imply that they were fat slobs,

☆ E.g., Billy Martin. ▶

it also suggested that they might be better off having one dainty little low-calorie beer. If that wasn't bad enough, the Gablinger's advertising had likewise failed to attract new beer drinkers. Would Meister Brau Lite besmirch McCann-Erickson's good name in the same way?

The second thing the McCann-Erickson people hated being saddled with was the name. Lite. Tacky, tacky. It made you think of blinking pink neon signs that said: "Nite Club! Girls Girls Girls." But if Miller was going to deep-six old Meister Brau, it liked Lite, and McCann-Erickson sighed and went to work. McCann-Erickson was not about to buck Miller. It was a growing account. When Philip Morris took over Miller, the company had only that tiny 4.2 percent market share. By 1973, with a younger, heartier image for High Life—"Miller Time!"—the brewery was well on its way to second place in the market and the 22.5 percent share it enjoys today. What could McCann-Erickson possibly do with the erstwhile Meister Brau Lite to avoid another Gablinger's?

There was one ray of hope. For reasons unknown to everyone (to this day), the town of Anderson, Indiana, was bonkers about Meister Brau Lite. Anderson—seat of Madison County, a nondescript industrial community of perhaps seventy thousand at the time—Anderson, Indiana, was crazy for Lite beer. Bill Backer, the creative director at McCann-Erickson, had put Bob Lenz, a creative group head, in charge of the Lite project, and for lack of anywhere else to turn, Lenz and a few others from the office bundled off to Anderson. There they toured the bars and watched rough-tough blue-collar workers wolf down Meister Brau Lites.

It would be nice to say that, inspired by this vision, Lenz and the other creative geniuses all said, as one: All we need to do is get ourselves some famous tough guys, just like these unknown types from Anderson, Indiana, and by showing that such he-men drink Lite, immediately stout and/or stout-hearted men across the length and breadth of this great land of ours will instantly begin storming bars and

package stores, demanding Lite Beer from Miller.

Alas, it didn't work out that way. While everyone from John Murphy—then president of Miller—on down credits Lenz with being the single individual most responsible for the campaign, Lenz himself is the first to admit that the Lite campaign was often more the beneficiary of serendipity. Some decisions were stumbled upon, others forced on Lite by its teeth-gnashing competitors. For example, although the first Lite commercial starred an athlete, and, as Lenz says, "as soon as we saw the audition tape we knew we had something," most of the subsequent early commercials turned to show-business characters. These commercials were often catch-as-catch-can. Lenz was working with a writer named Pacey Markham, and, Lenz recalls, "Pacey and I would make up endings as we were shooting."

Curiously, while Lite sales took off right away and accelerated so quickly that Miller had to move its timetable ahead, rolling the product out of test markets and onto a national platform way ahead of schedule, there was little disposition to credit the advertising. Lenz was not sure that it was working. "We got a lot of darts thrown at us," he recalls. Indeed, so different and allegedly unappealing was the campaign that many experts on Madison Avenue suspected it was just a tease, a preparation for the sustained drive yet to begin. "People would see me," Lenz says, "and they would actually ask me: 'Bob, when does the real campaign start?'"

But the ingredients were coming together. Markham had thought up the inspired ". . . and less" tag line early on. It was used in the first newspaper advertisement—a "positioning ad," so called—as indeed it has been used in every TV commercial, save No. 69, the 1981 Christmas group commercial (and even then the "and less" was there in Christmas spirit, with "and more" being wished for the holiday). Also, almost from the very beginning it was understood that Lite was a very different beer, and that therefore the commercials had to be very different, "no songs or cowboys." It also helped that John Murphy was willing, even anxious, to go along with a new tack. It is pretty much accepted that the commercials would not have turned so much to comedy were not the Miller president a man of such good humor himself.

Still, the problem remained that the Lite campaign had to go with facts. Not songs, not cowboys, not waterfalls, not waving grain—facts. And, as Lenz goes on, "What worried us was that people are talked *to* all the time on television. And now about beer? Facts about beer? The question was, who could we possibly get to deliver the message and make it interesting?"

And so it was that Bob Lenz was riding a bus in Manhattan one day. How would he know when he boarded that smelly vehicle that he was not just taking a ride uptown? No, he was beinning a Journey to Destiny. To this day, around the office, Lenz's associates say such things as, "Did you tell the bus story again, Bob?" Or: "Things still the same as ever on that bus ride, Bob?" Snide things like that. Keep in mind that these are the same sour types who would question whether Lana Turner was really discovered in Schwab's Drugstore.

But—vas you dere, Charlie?—Bob Lenz was on that bus, sitting there, jerking along, wondering about where the Lite campaign was going, when, as fate would have it, he happened to glance up at the little billboards that ringed the top of the bus interior. There, amid the messages for Preparation H, Anacin, cigarettes, and Eastern Airlines (in Spanish), was the smiling countenance of Matt Snell.

What a great face, what a great grin, Lenz thought. Of course, it tells us a lot about the thin reed of advertising that whereas Lenz was taken by Snell's face and instantly envisioned it being deployed on behalf of Lite Beer, he has no recollection of what it was that Snell was selling. In fact, as we know, it was Off-Track Betting, an enterprise that has gone from bad to worse in the intervening years since Mr. Snell was employed in its behalf.

Marty Blackman, for one, has no doubts that Lenz was inspired by the bus ad, but his recollection veers somewhat from the romantic get-me-Matt-Snell version. "The way I remember it," Blackman says, "it was mostly a case of: Snell was here. I'd worked with Matt before, so we knew he could do commercials. He was a good guy. He'd just retired; his name was still fresh. But, you know, he was convenient."

Snell, who grew up in the New York area, had been a college star for Woody Hayes at Ohio State; after nine years with the New York Jets he had just retired from the pros. He was on his way then to becoming a successful businessman—today he is president of Snellco, a construction company. He was also identified with a number of charitable and civic causes. As a player, he—not Joe Namath—had been the prime star of Super Bowl III, the most famous of them all, when the Jets upset the invincible Baltimore Colts in 1969. While Namath did all the talking, it was the taciturn Snell, rushing for 162 yards—a Super Bowl record that stood for a decade—who led the Jets to victory.

McCann-Erickson wooed Snell by sending him a case of Lite. To his surprise, he liked the beer and agreed to test for the commercial, thereby, as he admits with chagrin, assuring himself a place in the pantheon of sports history far above what anybody remembers him for accomplishing on the gridiron, even in the most famous Super Bowl of them all. Forever after, Matt Snell would be the answer to the trivia question: What athlete starred in the first Lite Beer commercial?

The historic event took place early in July of 1973, at a bar in Manhattan named Joe Allen's, which was rented for the occasion. If there was a script going in, it was used only as a reference point; it was to take the better part of three days for the shoot to obtain a thirty-second spot. "They really didn't know what they were looking for," Snell says, and Lenz doesn't dispute that. It was into the third day before "they got the right idea," Snell says. Then it only took a couple more hours to wrap it up. We can only let our imaginations run wild in speculating how dreadful the footage was that was rejected. The original—as well as almost all of the early commercials—seems downright primitive in comparison to what has evolved.

There is no humor as such in the Snell commercial, no sparkling lines, nothing original. It succeeds mostly in reinforcing what the bus ad had suggested to Lenz; that Matt Snell is a nice guy with a nice smile, and you certainly wouldn't mind having a few beers with him.

When the commercial opens, he is seated alone at a table, wearing a drab gray T-shirt, the graphics identifying him as

Matt Snell
Super Bowl Hero

The table is littered with empties, and a bunch of white guys are hanging around the bar in the background. And then Snell utters those immortal first words: "You know, new Lite Beer from Miller is all you ever wanted in a beer . . . and less."

He then goes on to enlighten us as to the properties of this new brew. It contains a third less calories, and it has fewer carbohydrates, too. Carbohydrates were very important to the early Lite advertising. There were books being written about carbohydrates at the time. It was a vital subject. Everybody in the early commercials went on and on about the carbohydrates. It was only after a time that they were dropped and "Less Filling" became the central theme in the saga.

"Less Filling was the key," Lenz says. "It was one of several ideas. I remember for a while we were thinking about going with Big Thirst. But luckily, we settled on Less Filling. If we hadn't, you and I wouldn't be talking about this today." Less Filling was a he-man's way of saying low-calorie, plus it hinted very strongly that you could drink a lot of the stuff.

After Snell holds up a bottle of Lite and explains its magic properties—with a camera zeroing in on a close-up of the bottle—a wide shot follows, with Snell offering something of a disclaimer. "Oh, I'm not saying I drank all this beer myself," he says, nodding at all the empties before him. "I had some help from my friends." The FTC required this explanation, and it is included in the first four Lite commercials. But the line doesn't intrude. It points out that not just Matt Snell, but everybody in the bar is drinking Lite, that the whole world is on its way to becoming one big Anderson, Indiana.

Then comes the rollicking punch line. Here it is. Snell says, "At six foot three, two-thirty, there's a lot of me to fill."

Not to be outdone, the guys at the bar shout back a clever rejoinder. It is: "Aw, come on!"

And so ends the first Lite Beer commercial. In the months that followed it appeared in a few scattered test markets around the country. History had been made, although no one was aware of it at the time.

Five Lites for the Doll

Although Matt Snell was a former athlete, there was no established policy that jocks would form the basis of the Lite campaign, and so, later that month, July 1973, the second commercial was shot with Mickey Spillane.

Frank Morrison Spillane is, of course, an author. Since 1946, when he dashed off *I, the Jury* in nineteen days, shocking a nation with its sex and violence (how well I, as a child, remember reading about all those "crisp, black triangles"), Spillane has written thirty-five mystery novels, which have sold in excess of seventy million volumes. He remains utterly unpretentious, however, and to this day prefers to think of himself as a "storyteller," instead of anything so highbrow as "writer" or "author." His works have appeared in every crevice of this globe. "All I know is, " Mickey said once, "that I'm one of the five most translated writers in the world. There's Tolstoy, Gorky, Jules Verne, somebody else, and me." The somebody else was Lenin.

Moreover—and especially for the purposes of Lite Beer commercials—Spillane was not only a name and a success, but he owned a distinct public image. In 1973, as in 1983—indeed, in every day of his life dating back to 1925 when Mickey was seven years old and growing up in Brooklyn—he has worn a crew cut. Moreover, even though most of Mickey's recent works have been award-winning children's books, he remains intermingled in the public mind with his most famous character: Mike Hammer, the no-nonsense, love-'em-and-leave-'em private dick first introduced in *I, the Jury*. Indeed, Mickey had once actually played Mike Hammer in a full-length movie.

To cover his whiffle cut, Mickey wore an old-fashioned fedora (just like Mike Hammer's) that looks rather like the meat-loaf sandwich Mickey talks about in a Lite commercial. Mickey was so identified with this chapeau that he used to hand hats out as gifts rather indiscriminately. However, since men generally stopped wearing hats in almost all places (except Lite Beer commercials) and certainly since they stopped favoring meat-loaf-sandwich fedoras, Mickey has had a hard time obtaining his signature hats, much less being able to dish them out. "You could never even find a hat like this in a place like California," he says. Instead, when he visits his old hometown of Gotham (which he hates) to shoot Lite commercials, he buys fedoras in lots, at sixty-five dollars a copy. "Can you believe that?" he asks. But then, people expect to see Mickey in a hat—that hat—just as they would expect Mike Hammer to wear one.

Perhaps there is no writer who, more than Spillane, has a persona that is so mixed in with one of his characters. Mick-

ey may be sort of what Ernest Hemingway wanted to be. Mickey was even, for a brief time, a professional athlete. After college at Fort Hays, Kansas, where he was on the swimming team, Spillane got a job swimming in aquacades for the Sheraton hotels. It's difficult to imagine Mickey in his burr cut paddling around in a fruity thing like an aquacade, but he has never fallen into any neat niche.

He had been in several commercials before Lite called. There was the Braniff one with Marianne Moore. Then Lifebuoy. And Piel's Beer at a time when they weren't going with Bert and Harry. His first commercial for Lite was the best of the early ones, and more significant too. Mickey came off from the outset as a definite character in his commercial, whereas Snell had been portrayed only as *a* jock. It took another year and a half before the agency began to understand this sufficiently—to present athletes as themselves, as distinct entities—first with Dick Butkus in May 1975, then with Rosie Grier, Boom-Boom Geoffrion, and Marv Throneberry. Only when the Spillane influence began to spread did the campaign become a true critical phenomenon.

In Spillane's first commercial, Lite No. 2, he is sitting in a bar, talking about this new beer, going on about the carbohydrates, assuring everybody that he didn't drink all the beer, that he had a little help from his friends (some thugs in the background), when Lee Meredith struts by, swinging a purse, jutting her remarkable breasts out, just as Mickey says: "What more would a man want on a long, lonely night?"

A Lite Beer, of course.

This commercial shoot went faster and smoother than Snell's, too. The only real problem the crew encountered was that it was an extremely hot summer's day in New York, and in the bar where they were shooting, the air-conditioning had been turned up all the way to counter the outside heat and the bright indoor camera lights. As a consequence Lee's nipples got very chilly and jutted out far too much for prime-time family viewing. Several good takes had to be thrown out before somebody finally went to her dressing quarters and advised her to cover the offending extremities with Band-Aids.

In the months that followed, as the campaign continued in test markets, half of the commercials were shot with show-business performers, not athletes. The one immediately following Mickey and the Doll's was shot with Ernie Stautner, an assistant football coach who had been All-Pro nine times with the Pittsburgh Steelers, and who was even more perfect for a beer commercial inasmuch as he had been born in Bavaria. But the next one was with Buddy Rich, the drummer, and after that, actors Sheldon Leonard and James Drury each had Lite commercials in the first year. Mickey's though, remained much the best of the early Lites.

Of course, Spillane has an advantage no other All-Star has, in that only he is regularly associated with Lee Meredith. He is so identified with her that if he makes an appearance for Lite without Lee, everyone says: "Hey, Mickey, where's the Doll?" By now Spillane, like so many of the sports All-Stars, is used to having become more famous for his commercials than for his real successes in life—he has heard many kids say "You write too?" when they find out about his books. But Mickey has the additional pleasant trauma of not even being appreciated for his commercials as a single.

One day, after a Lite shoot, Mickey and Bubba Smith were waiting at the airport in New York. A little old lady came up to them. "I know you," she said proudly.

"Yeah?" said Mickey.

"Sure. You're the big basketball player and you're the coach."

"See how famous we really are, Bubba?" Mickey sighed.

But he adores Lee. When the most recent Mike Hammer movie, *Murder Me, Murder You,* appeared on CBS last spring, Mickey made sure that Lee got a part. "She's a much better actress than they give her credit for," he says. He thinks she is discriminated against in that she is considered only for big-blonde parts. "The trouble is, they only see Lee when she dresses the part," Mickey says, "and they only want her for the same part all the time. She can cover them up if she has to. She can."

Maybe.

Probably the most dispassionate observation about Miss Meredith's upper anatomy came from Boog Powell, who was watching her take a few practice cuts last February for the softball commercial. "If I was pitching against Lee, I'd pitch her the same way they always pitched me," Boog observed. "They always tried to throw in on me, right under the broiler"—and he patted his big tummy. "Same with Lee. Pitch it in right under the tits." It was a very professional analysis.

Part of the ease Lee displays derives from her upbringing. "My father took a positive approach to sexiness," she says. "He was taking cheesecake photographs of me when I was two." Both her parents were schoolteachers, and she grew up in Fair Lawn, New Jersey. Lee's real name is Judith Lee Sauls, and the twig was bent early on. "I was built the same way I am now at the age of twelve," she explains. Indeed, it was about this time that she made one of her first stage appearances, playing in a school production of *Of Thee I Sing*. One of her lines was: "What does she have that I haven't got?" It got quite a laugh.

Lee was turned down in high school for membership in the dramatic club, but she toured as a precision dancer and was subsequently accepted at the American Academy of Dramatic Arts. Still, and notwithstanding what Mickey thinks she can do to conceal her most prominent assets, Lee has always been cast with them uppermost in mind. Her screen debut, for example, was as Ulla, the Swedish secretary, with Zero Mostel and Gene Wilder in *The Producers*. Later she gained a great deal of attention when she was featured as a sexy nurse in *The Sunshine Boys*, first on Broadway, then in the movies. She has, as well, been cast in more than one hundred commercials.

Everybody may call Lee Mickey's Doll or the Giggle Girl on the road, but in fact she is a shy housewife back in Jersey, happily married for thirteen years, with two daughters, Kim, twelve, and Erica, five. She won a Broadway contest for her cooking, but she is so stereotyped that Miller does not include her recipes in "The Lite All-Stars Food Favorites," a promotional booklet that lists the favorite dishes (all of which include some Lite Beer) of a select group of the heroes. These include:

☆ COUSY'S CREAMY COLESLAW (*made with 1/3 cup Lite*)
☆ BUBBA'S CHICKEN SOUPER BOWL (*6 cups Lite*)
☆ SAUSAGES à la BOOM-BOOM (*1½ cups Lite*)
☆ MARVELOUS MARV'S MACARONI SALAD (*½ cup Lite*)
☆ DEACON'S SLOPPY JOES (*one 12-ounce can Lite*)
☆ DON CARTER'S SPARE RIBS (*¾ cup Lite*)
☆ MICKEY'S MYSTERY MEAT LOAF
  (*1/3 cup Lite in the Bar B.Q. Sauce*)
☆ JOHN MADDEN'S HALF-TIME BAKED HAM
  (*one 12-ounce can Lite*)
☆ BUTKUS'S BUBBLING BEEF STEW (*5 cups Lite*)
☆ BOOG'S BEER BISCUITS (*1 cup Lite*)

Lee also exercises and jogs regularly. "Aw," says Mickey, "she doesn't need that. Some people are just built." He still looks after Lee in an avuncular way. Altogether, Mickey has brought the Doll to eleven commercials. He has been in twelve. The only time Lee missed working with Mickey was for the tug-o'-war commercial, which was shot on the beach at Pompano, Florida, early in 1978. Lee was pregnant with Erica at the time. It is a measure of her uniqueness and how much Lite values her that instead of getting a substitute to take her place, *two* girls were hired in Lee's stead.

None of the All-Stars are leading men. Instead, they are all character actors, tending toward humorous self-deprecation. As Spillane points out with chagrin, the reason why Mickey and the Doll works so well is because he is so much older than Lee—at sixty-five, Mickey is the second oldest All-Star, a few months younger than Jim Honochick—so nobody takes the liaison as anything but burlesque. Were Lee to be paired in any sort of romantic way—even comically—with one of the younger, better-looking All-Stars, it just wouldn't work.

Traditionally, of course, it has been understood that hotshot athletes get the girls, and so it is probably one of the charms of the series that the Lite All-Stars don't score. Essentially, the Lite line is men in groups, not men chasing women. Lee is ogled, never chased.

Surely it is no coincidence that by far the worst Lite commercial ever aired was completely out of character. In this one, shot in the fall of 1976, Paul Hornung, the Golden Boy, strides down a gridiron, determined to make Narcissus jealous. "See this face?" Hornung asks. "It's gorgeous." And so on. Then he is mobbed by cheerleaders, who descend on him and wrestle him to the ground.

If you never saw this commercial, it is because McCann-Erickson regained its wits and yanked it after only one or two showings. Hornung subsequently made another commercial with the same theme, that he is irresistible to women, but at least this one has a good tag line: "Practice, practice, practice." Even better, that line was turned to real advantage some months later, in the Great Lite Beer Shoot-out, when Steve Mizerak cleans the table and walks off with the Doll. "Steve, how do you do that?" Hornung asks.

"Practice, practice, practice," Steve replies, turning the tables on the Golden Boy. Here was where Hornung's role obviously lay with Lite: the handsome, self-assured bounder who *loses* the girl to lesser guys. But after a brief cameo in the next Alumni commercial, the Golden Boy left the All-Stars in a dispute over money.

Actually, apart from the Doll, women seldom appear in the commercials, and almost never as sex symbols or love interests. Rodney, of course, gets put down. The only other star to try and get something going in a commercial is Wilt Chamberlain, in his one Lite. To a pretty young woman at the bar, he says: "Hey, babe, what's going on?" But we don't find out how that gambit fares, because just then the gigantic bartender comes over and *he* puts Wilt down—calling him "Shorty"—before the lady has a chance to respond to Wilt's advance.

LEFT TO RIGHT: *Lee Meredith, Ray Nitschke, Don Carter, and Boog Powell*

Three waitresses pop up in the sagas—with Ernie Stautner in Lite No. 3, Dick Butkus in No. 10, and Bruce Wilhelm in No. 45. In the Sheldon Leonard commercial, No. 6, a moll in a red dress does her fingernails, and in the Joe Frazier musical comedy, No. 30, some of the singers are female. The two girls do the beach walk in place of the Doll in No. 34, and some of the Dallas Cowboy Cheerleaders are momentarily glimpsed through binoculars in Lite No. 76. Otherwise, apart from Lee's eleven appearances, that's it. Women are never part of the bar extras.

Increasingly, there has been a hue and cry that Lite should shoot a commercial with a former female athlete. The issue is discussed regularly, but so far the agency and the brewery have both rejected the idea. There are several reasons. Part of the problem is simply that there are few former female athletes who are well known. Moreover, most of the famous ones are in golf and tennis, and they still remain active in some manner, just as older male golfers and tennis players do.

To get around that, it has been suggested that a female entertainer be used instead—ideally someone with a bawdy image. In fact, a commercial based on that premise was written years ago and is still lying around. In it, the woman would talk about how there has never been a lady who's done a Lite Beer commercial, and then at the end, with a come-on, she would say: "And believe me, they still haven't gotten the first *lady*."

The consensus on that idea is that it might cause more problems than it would solve. Ultimately, however, the reason there has never been a commercial shot with a woman in the leading role is that there is more of a commercial risk in trying that than in continuing to go along with a successful campaign that engenders only a small amount of criticism. "Look," Lee says, "it's all such a joke. But I also appreciate that some women can't see the humor and are offended."

Late in 1982, Lite No. 76, featuring Dallas Cowboys Charlie Waters and D. D. Lewis, showed a brief shot of less than two seconds of the Cowboy Cheerleaders. Anybody who watches any football game on television will see more provocative shots, of cheerleaders and spectators alike, but the Cowboy Cheerleaders represent an anti-female image to many women, and a significant number of complaints were delivered to Miller—enough for the brewery to yank the commercial.

The number of women offended by any of the Lite commercials is small, however. Research shows that women continue to drink Lite, as sure as they understand the commercials and enjoy them. Indeed, it is estimated that 50 percent of Lite beer drinkers are female, although in keeping with the usual beer-drinking pattern, wherein a small number of drinkers consume most of the beer, that 50 percent of female drinkers puts away only 30 percent of the Lite volume. Beer-drinking's image among women has been enhanced precisely because of the light brands; similarly, light-beer drinkers tend to be more upscale than those who order the same old two-fisted brews.

One reason why Lee Meredith is so widely accepted by almost all viewers of both sexes is that her Lite character is so broad a caricature that it is impossible to take her seriously. Nor is she alone. The Lite commercials are jammed with stereotypes, replete with famous people laughing at themselves. Almost everybody in them is somewhat stereotyped. When I agreed☆ to do the sportswriter commercial, a few of my colleagues asked me if I didn't think I was somehow denigrating myself and the profession. Are you kidding? If an umpire can laugh at himself for having poor eyesight, am I going to stand on some kind of ceremony? "I'm not going to change the world," Jim Honochick says. "How many times did I walk into a ballpark and they played 'Three Blind Mice'? It's just fun." In fact, I would submit that a lot of fans have a

warmer feeling toward umps now for having seen Honochick laugh at himself. In a way, the stereotyping is so obvious, so *stereotyped*, that possibly it helps us reject those stereotypes in future. You can laugh some things to death better than you can wipe them out in more serious ways.

And so everything is fair game: not just the blind umpire and the sexy blond. A big, dumb black man named Bubba. Stupid musclemen. Coaches without discipline. A kamikaze Japanese. Foolish cops. Lying fishermen. Good-for-nothing surfers. Marv Throneberry.

Even whole sports are satirized. Hockey players are violent cretins. Tennis is effete. Bowling is lower class. "This is going to set my sport back twenty years," Don Carter laughed, as he watched bowling lanes being transformed into a smokey dive. In a way, Lite Beer even makes fun of itself, and we love it for that.

Pitch her under the tits.

☆   Agreed isn't quite the right word. "Leapt at it" may be more accurate.

A Six-Pack to Go

Despite the increasingly favorable attention the Lite commercials began to enjoy as the campaign passed through its second year, as the brand was rushed into national distribution, something was still lacking. "We just hadn't found a groove yet," Bob Lenz says. Bob Meury, a vice-president at McCann-Erickson who became the main writer early on, says, "We were too cautious with the athletes. With somebody like Spillane we'd play around more." Of the first eight commercials aired, four used show-biz people instead of athletes, and one early one, starring a black comedian named Scoey Mitchlll, was shot but not used. The campaign was still flying by the seat of its

pants. "We would make up the endings as we were shooting," Lenz recalls.

To be fair, in those days of yore, more information about the beer itself had to be included in the thirty seconds. The carbohydrates, for example. What is this thing called Lite? Nowadays everybody knows what a light beer is, so the commercials can focus on being self-contained acts, with only a passing reference to the beer's ingredients and other qualities required. Also, in those early times the characters—the athletes—themselves were often new as national personalities, and some time had to be spent introducing them.

Consider, for example, how patently impossible it would

have been to have made a commercial such as the Friday Night Lite Beer Card Game (which was shot in 1982) in the early going. This thirty-second spot is a whole repertory theater—Boog Powell, Jim Shoulders, Koichi Numazawa, Mickey and the Doll—and if so much as a second had had to be devoted to explaining who these characters were and what they represented, there wouldn't have been enough time for the laughs, much less for Boog to plug Lite. The climax, following Boog's remark, "All right, Numa, cut the cards," with Numa "cutting" them by splitting the table with an Oriental chop, is funny mostly because we have seen Numa do that before. Indeed, we start to laugh in anticipation even before he goes into action.

The early commercials had none of this range. Moreover, there was dead time in the middle of each, when a close-up of the bottle was shown. This was for two reasons. First, it was considered important to let everybody see this new wonder beer, and,

The Friday Night
Lite Beer Card Game

second, nobody at the agency had any real faith that athletes could act their way through a whole thirty seconds straight—or even twenty-six or so, not counting the obligatory product shot, which invariably appeared at the end. If the close-up was shown in the middle, then the editors could use the best of one take for the opening, patching it up with the best of another take for the second half. But to achieve this better choice and higher quality, a certain amount of continuity was lost in the middle of the drama.

The ninth Lite commercial, shot early in 1975, featured Dave DeBusschere, late of the championship New York Knicks. DeBusschere had retired to become general manager of the New York Nets of the American Basketball Association, and he was a revered figure in New York, the athlete *cum* executive, all of that. No doubt for these reasons, the commercial with De Busschere is perhaps the drabbest of any shot, with all the charm of a commercial for old people's insurance featuring Lorne Green or Ed McMahon. DeBusschere's big scene takes place in a locker room (curiously, still the only Lite commercial shot in such an obvious location), but about all it contains is a worshipful shot of DeBusschere chucking an empty Lite can into a wastebasket. And he makes it as we hear fans cheer! It's a complete yawn. The carbohydrates are the best part of this commercial.

Ironically, everything changed with the next Lite—the first time Miller used athletes back-to-back in the campaign. The call went out to Blackman for a tough old football player, and he suggested three retired linebackers: Sam Huff, ex-New York Giant, as sainted in Gotham as was DeBusschere; Joe Schmidt, who had anchored the great Detroit Lion teams of the fifties; and Dick Butkus, a rugged 250-pounder who had made All-Pro in his seven seasons with the Chicago Bears, a linebacker who always receives considerable recognition as the best in history at his position.

For no particular reason, Butkus was called to New York to audition first. When he was finished, Schmidt and Huff were forgotten. Butkus was a natural. His commercial was not only going to change the Lite campaign, it was also going to change his life. After retiring from pro football (and subsequently suing the Bears for not looking after his best medical interests), Butkus had worked in Florida for Nautilus, the physical exercise equipment company. Eventually he was to give up a business career, move to Los Angeles, and try to make it as an actor. Butkus has appeared in a number of TV series, as well as in a couple of movies, has shot a TV pilot that stars him in the role of a sheriff, and is also considering a script that would feature all ex-athletes in the main male roles. Besides, Butkus has now appeared in thirteen Lite commercials, passing Mickey and the Doll to take the lead for the most appearances in the campaign.

The interesting thing about Butkus, too, is that of all the All-Stars, his role, his persona, is really the only one to have

Mr. Butkus and Mr. Smith
Famous Lite Beer drinkers

changed in the commercials over the years. He is introduced in 1975 as a belligerent meanie, a dummy to boot, but as time passes, and especially once he starts teaming up with Bubba Smith (beginning in the summer of 1979), Butkus evolves not only into a straight man, but into a rather intelligent and patient figure, who is tolerant and forgiving in putting up with the bumbling Bubba. It is certainly significant that in the serious Christmas commercial of 1981, it was Butkus who was the All-Star selected to set the tone by delivering the opening message.

What started Dick Butkus on his way as an actor was Lite No. 10, which was set in a bowling alley. The commercial, frankly, isn't all that clever. It consists of little more than Butkus trying to convince the assembled bowlers and an especially skeptical waitress that despite his reputation as a rugged football player, he isn't all that bad a guy—it's really no more than an extension of the primitive Snell and Stautner big-guy routines. "Most people think I'm a real monster," Butkus says. "But actually, I'm very sensitive." At the end he bowls like a monster, and the commercial ends with the bottle in the product shot shaking. That's pretty

Dick Butkus

Ben Davidson

much it. Except that, for the first time an athlete has laughed at himself. The tone has been set; an "attitude" established.

"Attitude" is the favorite word of Bob Giraldi, who is recognized as one of the two must successful commercial directors in the business—the other being Joe Settemeyer, best known for his Federal Express commercials. It is no coincidence that the Butkus commercial, Lite No 10, was the first one Giraldi was called on to direct—or that he would go on to handle three quarters of the commercials shot for Lite since then.

With Butkus, everything came together. The commercials that followed only got funnier. In the next one, Lite found its comedian, Rodney Dangerfield, telling us, "I finally found a beer I can respect," but after that McCann-Erickson went

back to the jocks, using Rosie Grier, another big football-player, doing needlework—a hobby he had received a lot of publicity for—along with two other ex-grid behemoths, Ray Nitschke and Ben Davidson. Next, Mickey and the Doll made their first reprise, and then Boom-Boom Geoffrion, the old hockey star, was chosen to do a new slant on the Butkus number, with a whole hockey team—uniforms, sticks, and all—crashing into the bar after him. The pattern of humorous self-criticism was set by the Lite heroes just as the beer was launched into the national market. At this point, early in 1976, the whole concept of a low-calorie beer was still new to most Americans. Today, only seven years later, about one out of every six beers sold in the U.S. is a light beer, and far more than half of those are Lites.

I'll Get
Seven Lites
After This Inning

The burgeoning Lite sales caught most other beer companies by surprise. Despite all evidence to the contrary, they continued to believe that Lite would do another Gablinger's. "The most amazing thing of all," says Barry Barrett, the Lite brand manager at Miller, "is that it was a full year before any other major beer even put a light in test market." That was Schlitz. Anheuser-Busch was even more of a sleeping giant, and it would be yet another year before it finally began to crank up Natural Light.

When Schlitz entered the competition as Lite's first rival, it focused its advertising on taste, suggesting that, okay, Lite might be acceptable with calories and carbohydrates, but it wasn't much to the palate. This was somewhat ironic, because it was during the seventies that regular Schlitz went from being the clear national runner-up to Bud down to a position where it struggles to stay in the top five. And this decline was strictly on account of taste; the brewery decided to change Schlitz's formula. The new Schlitz included more corn syrup and a less expensive barley malt, with the resulting product so radically different—and evidently so inferior, too—that it even got tagged as "green beer," meaning that it didn't taste as if it had been aged enough.

It was after this disastrous decision that Miller High Life, a lowly seventh when purchased by Philip Morris, shot past Schlitz—also going by Pabst, which more and more got saddled with the sissy image that Miller had once owned.☆ As local beers fell by the wayside, image counted more and more. As High Life moved up and Lite caught on, so did one other brand make a big move: Coors.

For long only a regional brand in the West, Coors began to take on a mystical image. People like Paul Newman and President Ford were supposed to fly in cases of Coors from Colorado, so they could enjoy the beer whenever they were located outside the market territory. Coors became a cult beer and climbed up with the national leaders.☆☆ Ironically, though, Coors lost some of its mystique as its availability widened. Obviously, part of its success had been that it was forbidden fruit, and as soon as it could be obtained in other parts of the country, its charm diminished. Then the beer was forced to suffer the sins of its owners. The Coors family was publicized for its espousal of many far-right causes, the company was accused of being anti-black, anti-Hispanic, and anti-woman, and overnight, in many quarters, it became a statement *not* to drink Coors. Paul Newman switched to Bud, which helps sponsor his racing car.

But, while most beers have had some jagged sales charts at one time or another, Lite has suffered no real setbacks. Indeed, starting with the Schlitz light attack in 1976, it has tended to prosper in the face of competition.

It was Schlitz that forced McCann-Erickson to move the Lite advertising to a more sophisticated and entertaining level: the Less Filling/Tastes Great debates. Spillane was chosen to break the ice with his second commercial, putting on his hat and trenchcoat, pausing on a dark street outside a

bar to say of Lite: "I started drinking it because I heard it was less filling. I kept on drinking it because it tastes great." But nobody showed up to argue with Mickey—just the Doll to say, "Hey, Mickey, got a Lite?" It was Lite No. 15, shot in March 1976, that first utilized the LF/TG argument.

Bob Meury was primarily responsible for this new concept, although what made it work immediately were the two debaters chosen for the initial argument commercial: Tommy Heinsohn, then the coach of the Boston Celtics, and Mendy Rudolph, for years the premier official in the National Basketball Association. The script called for a coach and a ref to be arguing in the bar about the merits of Lite. When the coach will not agree that it is first of all less filling, the ref gives him the heave-ho sign, yanking his thumb and screaming, "You're out of the bar."

The commercial was shot early in the spring, when pro basketball was moving toward its annual climax, but even if it had been another season, the choice of sport was felicitous. Meury is a big basketball fan, and he recognized that basketball coaches are the most visible in their profession, much closer to the fans than baseball managers or football coaches. Indeed, not long before Lite approached Heinsohn,

Tommy Heinsohn vs. Mendy Rudolph

☆   But let's not forget the finest beer song of this or any other era, a country-and-western classic of a patriotic nature that was an ode to "rednecks, white shirts, and Blue Ribbon beer."

☆☆   It is fourth in sales today, after Bud, High Life, and Lite, just ahead of Pabst and Michelob.

Boog Powell and Jim Honochick

he had complained to the NBA league office that he was too exposed, that the television cameras were intruding too closely, focusing on him so carefully when he argued with officials that it was possible for viewers to read his lips. "That's why this thing first came up that I'm a nut," he says plaintively.

But if basketball coaches are more recognizable than their peers in other sports, basketball referees are the absolute cynosures of their profession. Jim Honochick, a retired baseball umpire who was to become—after Mendy Rudolph—the second official to appear in the Lite campaign, umpired in the American League for a quarter of a century, appearing in seven All-Star games and six World Series, but, he says, right up until the day he retired, and even after he might have been involved in a rhubarb with the home club, Honochick could walk out of any stadium, waltz straight through an angry crowd, and never be spotted. No one had the foggiest idea who he was until he made the blind umpire commercial with Boog Powell in 1978. Then, instantly, wherever Honochick appeared, people would scream out "Hey, you're Boog Powell!"

But anybody who'd ever seen an NBA game, live or on TV, knew Mendy Rudolph. Indeed, just like certain superstar players—Reggie, say, or Moses, or Billie Jean—there came to be only one Mendy in sports, and he was known by just his first name; i.e., "Strom, Vanak, Garretson, and Mendy will be working the finals." Like other distinctive basketball officials who preceded him, men such as Sid Borgia or Charley Eckman, Mendy was a ham with a highly personal style. He was also the most fastidious of officials, and when kids imitated him—yes, kids imitated an official; they imitated Mendy—they would more often than not do his famous brow-wipe, in which he would throw off an offending drop of sweat with the middle finger of his right hand. Mendy also used a handkerchief better than anybody in athletics. He had a great deal of style, and he delighted in the additional notoriety he received from the Lite commercials in the three years he had left to live. (Mendy is still the only All-Star to die.) It was a compliment for an official to be included in such company, and he was proud of that.

Mendy and Heinsohn were distinctive in another way: they were the first athletic personalities chosen who were still active in sports and in the public eye☆ at the time they shot their commercials. Other coaches or managers who have been on display since they made a Lite commercial include: Boom-Boom Geoffrion, K. C. Jones, Randy Marsh, Don Nelson, Whitey Herzog, Dick Williams, Billy Martin, and Frank Robinson. Le Roy Jolley remains an active horse trainer, and Steve Mizerak continues to compete in championship pool events because pool is not considered a sport. No one, though, was so visible at his athletic specialty while qualifying as an All-Star as was Mendy.

Heinsohn, though more of an unknown dramatic quality,

☆ Ernie Stautner had been an assistant football coach at the time he shot Lite No. 3, but only All-Pro offensive football linemen are more anonymous than assistant football coaches.

was a fortunate choice, and arguably, to this day, remains the best acting athlete in the series. How many All-American athletes, for example, were prominent members of their high school drama club?

At parochial school in northern New Jersey (not far from where Lee Meredith would be turned down by her school drama society), Heinsohn was an impressive young thespian. On one occasion he was denied school permission to play in an all-star basketball game, because he was considered more valuable to the school on the stage, where he had been selected to play the butler in *The Student Prince.* On another occasion, when young Heinsohn was carrying 130 pounds on a six-foot-four-inch frame—and before his husky cigarette voice had fully mellowed—he played a role onstage in drag.

Lite was not aware of Heinsohn's early training, nor that he had already appeared in several other commercials. One, for a clothing store in Philadelphia named Boyd's, had won an award. In that, Heinsohn had begun: "I used to hate to come to Philadelphia, because all anybody would say to me was, 'Hey, Heinsohn, you big bum.' " Then he went on to explain that at six feet seven inches, 250 pounds, he was hard to outfit, but he had finally found a classy store like Boyd's. And, he concludes: "Now when I come to Philadelphia, people say: 'Hey, Heinsohn, you big bum, where did you get that nice suit?' " Heinsohn was so good they used the first take.

Since being introduced to America in the Lite commercials, Heinsohn has picked up a Hollywood agent and has been urged to move to Tinseltown. He was cast in one TV pilot in one of the lead roles (as, of all things, a *football* coach), but Heinsohn has always lived in the northeast and retains a number of interests there. Heinsohn is the only All-Star who has ever been fired by another All-Star, ☆ but he continues as one of the Celtics' broadcasters (Cousy is another), he sells insurance, and belying his public image as a nut, he is a recognized landscape artist who has had exhibitions in galleries in both Boston and New York. He is also among a growing number of modern athletes who supplement their income by giving motivational speeches to industry.

Heinsohn has been used by Lite in a number of commercials since his debut with Mendy—being asked, with Butkus, to manage the greatest range—but the LF/TG argument itself remains a staple shtick that has barely been modified since Heinsohn and Mendy first went at it. It has served as the theme of most of the Alumni Commercials, of course, but let us also walk down memory lane with the likes of Butkus and the rugby player (Mike Roberts); the Van Arsdales; Boom-Boom and Jacques Plante, arguing in French; Billy "I Feel Strongly Both Ways" Martin; Martin and George Steinbrenner (twice, yet); the Quarry brothers; Boog and Numa.

All right, it's less filling.

☆ Red Auerbach canned him from the Celtic job in 1978.

Eight Lites for the Boys

in the Back Room

If it was Schlitz Light that spurred Lite to new advertising heights, it was Budweiser that was directly responsible for creating the All-Star program. As the beer business has consolidated, the giants have taken a larger and larger share of the market, and the battle lines between the two are always drawn. Together Anheuser-Busch and Miller sell well over half the beer in America, with Budweiser the Number One brand, trailed by High Life and Lite at place and show.

A-B, as Anheuser-Busch is always referred to in the trade, is even more of a juggernaut in sports advertising, the most popular place to tout beer. Deals change from year to year,

but of all the major-league teams in the country—baseball, football, basketball, and hockey—A-B sponsors about two thirds of the franchises. In baseball, which has by far the most games, Bud has a drumbeat across the summer beer-drinking season, ☆ sponsoring twenty of the twenty-six teams. Miller has tie-ins with the rest, except, of all people, with its hometown Milwaukee Brewers, who are sponsored by Pabst. As much as Miller has grown since Philip Morris took it over—August Busch III has been known privately to

☆ Fully one third more beer is sold May through August than November through February.

disparage the Miller management as "tobacco people"—Budweiser remains the industry leader, a powerful and wise competitor.

Indeed, A-B's only major goof in a long time was in the way it handled the low-calorie line. First, it reacted late to the obvious demand Miller had demonstrated for a lighter beer, and then when A-B finally did respond by bringing out Natural Light, it made the bizarre advertising decision to mirror the Lite campaign, using ex-athletes to do funny bits in saloons. Apparently the thinking was that if Natural ads were similar to Lite ads, doubt would be sown, drinkers would get confused, figure that all light beers were the same, and not really care whether they ordered a Lite or a Natural. To buttress this plan, A-B decided to go one step further. It would not only use some retired athletes of its own—Catfish Hunter, Gordie Howe, Walt Frazier—but it would try and steal some of Lite's jocks away.

Up to this point there was no Lite program that was organized for its TV stars. Guy did a commercial, got paid, that was pretty much it. A few Lite principals had made appearances for the brewery over the years, but that was a catch-as-catch-can sort of thing. As early as 1977 several of the Lite players had been assembled for what came to be known as the Alumni commercials, but that was also considered to be a one-shot deal at the time. In fact, the next year, when Miller decided that it wanted another group commercial, it was such an afterthought that when the tug-o'-war idea was agreed upon, it was very difficult to find a place at the beach in prime season that could accommodate all the talent and the production staff. Finally Blackman found a spa in Pompano Beach, Florida. Even worse, Lee Meredith was pregnant, so Lite viewers missed the opportunity to see her in a bathing suit. Talk about bad planning.

The next year, 1979, came the banquet commercial, and by now the Alumni shoot was accepted as an annual event, but still, it remained a relatively low-key exercise. No effort was made to bring in the press, and while there was a banquet for the commercial there was no real banquet—or any other sort of formal gathering—for the stars.

Lite never bought its loyalty either. Compared to some campaigns, in which perhaps one or two, maybe three celebrities were paid huge sums of money, endorsement contracts for the Lite heroes were relatively modest. The principle was established early on, too, that payment would be fairly equal, in the nature of a team sharing a playoff pool, where the superstars and substitutes all get the same amount. For the Alumni shoots, everyone gets exactly the same (around $12,500), and for the regular thirty-second spots the starting fees are not a great deal higher. "Payment is much closer than anyone wants to imagine," Marty Blackman says. It does go up some for repeat performances, thereby, in effect, rewarding fairly those whose first commercial scores well enough for them to merit a return.

A few stars, such as Wilt Chamberlain and Rosie Grier, have refused to do subsequent commercials, feeling that the price just wasn't right. Paul Hornung was dropped for agitating for higher pay for everyone, stirring up a fuss at an Alumni shoot. Others, notably Archie Moore and Sugar Ray Robinson, turned down invitations to do Lite commercials because they considered the pay scale inferior.

LEFT TO RIGHT: Steve Mizerak, John Madden, and Dick Butkus

But all along the reverse has been much more common, with retired athletes anxious to gain the money, exposure, prestige, and fun that comes with a Lite shot. Indeed, Blackman, the agency, and Miller are regularly petitioned by forgotten old heroes, pleading for an audition. It is surely well understood now that Lite can produce more fame than a mere sports career ever did. Typical is John Madden, who laughs and says: "Hell, I'd been around. I was a Super Bowl coach. How many times was I on national television, marching up and down the sidelines? But never mind. I coached for twenty years, I *won* the Super Bowl, but I'll be known forever as the guy who breaks through the paper."

Apart from simple pecuniary considerations, there were three other defections. Both Brooks Robinson and Whitey Herzog took baseball jobs—Robinson as an announcer, Herzog went on to lead the A-B Cardinals to a World Series win in 1982 over the Milwaukee Brewers in the battle of the beers. In a somewhat different case, Whitey Ford made the mistake of promoting a boutique beer known as Hall Of Fame, but he has returned to the fold to some extent, inasmuch as he gave Miller permission to use his name in Bob Uecker's second commercial, Lite No. 79. (Joe DiMaggio was the original name in the script, but whereas it could be borrowed to use with the likes of Mrs. Robinson, Joe D wouldn't permit its commercial use.)

And so the affiliation to Lite may have remained a loose, often short-term one, but then Bud entered the fray. Natural went after some of the Lite players, waving checkbooks, offering double what Miller had paid for commercials. Three of the Lite stars—Mickey Mantle, Joe Frazier, and Nick Buoniconti—took the money and jumped. A-B was ecstatic. One executive in St. Louis actually crowed that "this was the greatest defection since Solzhenitsyn." A Natural commercial was specifically written to call attention to the turncoats. Norm Crosby, a comedian who became the Natural spokesman—himself an acquired taste who talks in mala-

propisms—cried out to Mantle: "Hey, you switched. I thought you were enameled with that other light beer."

The Natural commercials were not artistically bad, but hovering over them all was the scent of staleness, the hint of damaged goods. Miller and its agency were flabbergasted that A-B had chosen this curious tack, but they grew secretly pleased when their polling showed that beer drinkers resented the copycat commercials and, especially, the Lite trio who had sold out to the other brand. Bob Meury says: "Those commercials just didn't understand beer drinkers. If there's one thing a guy is who drinks beer—he's fair."

Natural floundered while Lite continued to prosper, until, finally, A-B went to the bullpen in 1982 for a new entry, Bud Light. Natural was not put on waivers, merely sent down to the minors as a so-called "popular priced" brand, like Busch or Old Milwaukee. (Bud, High Life, Lite, and now Bud Light are known in the trade as premiums, while Michelob and Lowenbrau are called super-premiums. There are no cheap beers anymore, only cheap drinkers.) It was estimated that A-B's start-up costs for Bud Light would exceed $50 million, which sounds like a great deal of money, but in a country that spends in excess of $30 billion a year for beer, with light beer consumption obviously here to stay, that is small potatoes for a company like A-B just to get into the game. Once a brand is nationally established now, the profit-per-container increases dramatically the more cans or bottles are sold. Indeed, past a certain point it costs more to buy the containers and market the product than it does to brew the beer that goes in the container.

But if Natural Light has faded into the background, its legacy will forever be that it brought the All-Stars into existence for Lite. As soon as the word got out that Natural was wooing a lot of the All-Stars and had indeed won some of them over, Lite galvanized for action. An emergency meeting was convened in Milwaukee, with the brewery flying out a large agency contingent from New York. The atmosphere was heightened because it had been only recently that Miller had switched agencies, withdrawing its business from McCann-Erickson and giving it to a new firm, Backer & Spielvogel. The people involved were almost all the same—Carl Spielvogel had been vice-chairman at McCann, and Lenz and Meury had also come over with the account—but Backer & Spielvogel depended heavily on Miller.

Out of this crisis came the establishment of the formal All-Star program, with a full-time director. The All-Stars—there are thirty-six of them now—are not salaried Miller employees, but many of them do receive guarantees. In return, they must make a specified number of personal appearances. Some of these are in-house—pepping up distributors and salesmen, touring the breweries. Occasional seminars are conducted in Milwaukee, in order to give the All-Stars at least a working knowledge about beer and the beer business. Other times the All-Stars make speeches, attend charity functions, serve as grand marshals in parades, that sort of thing. Ben Davidson, who has appeared at everything from the Indy 500 to the Mardi Gras, points out: "The great thing to keep in mind is that pretty much everywhere you go, it's a celebration. There's nothing more fun than being a VIP when everybody is happy."

Some effort is made to spread the assignments around, but, obviously, all All-Stars are not equal. Likewise, not all have the same capabilities, and only certain ones could work commencements and ordinations. Boom-Boom Geoffrion does far and away the most number of appearances for Lite, thirty-five or forty a year, "everything but nightclubs," but Boom-Boom doesn't really count because he is the only one of the All-Stars who works full-time for Miller. As the only Hispanic on the team, Palomino, the youngest All-Star, has a heavy schedule in the Southwest, and some effort is made to hand out the assignments on a regional basis, but Boog Powell holds the record, traveling all the way from his home in Key West, Florida, to make an appearance in Alaska.

Boom-Boom Geoffrion

Carlos Palomino and Tommy Heinsohn

Rarely do the All-Stars grouse about their affiliation with Miller. Most, in fact, genuinely treasure it and remain grateful that they have been given this additional day in the sun. It is also true that the All-Stars are, for the most part, an exceptionally nice collection of middle-aged men. Rarely is a Bad Guy selected, for the simple reason that this is a personality team, and so there's no need to choose rotten eggs in the first place or put up with one if a mistake is made.

"This really is a very compatible group of men," Ray Nitschke says. He still lives in the Green Bay area, where he works as a manufacturer's representative for a trucking company. "Given all the egos and backgrounds involved that may be very unusual, but the truth is, we all seem to have great respect for each other. Apart from the money and everything else you gain by being an All-Star, I genuinely look forward to getting together every year—and I know the other guys feel the same way. I know it sounds corny, but in one sense it really is just like being on a team."

At least in terms of recognition, virtually all of the All-Stars have been affected by appearing in the commercials. And while it is difficult to measure this sort of thing qualitatively, it would seem that at least three of the All-Stars have had their lives greatly changed by the commercials. These are, not surprisingly, three men who had enjoyed less of a taste of fame before they began appearing in the commercials: Jim Honochick, Steve Mizerak, and—who else?—Marv Throneberry.

Honochick was retired from umpiring and doing public relations work for the First National Bank of Allentown (Pennsylvania), where he has lived all his life, when he was called for an audition by Lite. Honochick had never achieved any notoriety. Controversy was not his style. Boog Powell suggests one reason why their commercial—one of the most popular of all—worked so well. "Jim and I were a lot alike on the field," Boog says. "We both just went out and did our jobs without a lot of fuss."

Honochick had been a ballplayer himself after he graduated from Temple University, but he never rose any higher than Triple A—although, ironically, he played at that level with the minor-league forerunner of Powell's team, the Orioles. Honochick was about to be called up to the bigs, but the war changed everything, and one day in July 1946, after he had come back from the service to Baltimore, he was shaving—and he looked at himself in the mirror, and suddenly it hit him. "Why don't you become an umpire?" he said, out loud. To this day, Honochick has "not the slightest idea" why this thought suddenly entered his mind. He was only twenty-nine at the time, batting .289. The team general manager was flabbergasted when Honochick revealed this inspiration to him. "Are you crazy, Jim?" he thundered. "No man with a college education ever wanted to be an umpire." But Honochick was determined. Within a week he was umpiring a Class D game in Milford, Delaware, and he was obviously such a natural that within two and a half years he was in the majors, there to stay for twenty-five years, watched by millions—in anonymity.

Honochick shot his first Lite, No. 37, in August 1978, and three months later Mizerak got his chance. This is the one where he makes the trick pool shot, and then says, ". . . even when you're just showing off. . ." He had been tested for the commercial against three other pool players, and while Mizerak had won all sorts of honors in pool—four straight U.S. Opens, a record 321 straight balls, the youngest person ever inducted into the billiards Hall of Fame—Mizerak was totally unknown outside of the pool community, and had, in fact, been supporting his family as a schoolteacher since 1968. At the time he was chosen "in happy disbelief" to make the Lite ad, Steve was teaching seventh-grade social studies in Perth Amboy, New Jersey.

Since the commercial, Mizerak has become famous enough to abandon the classroom and work pool full-time. Thus he surely profits directly from the exposure more than any other Lite star. The Lite commercials have made Mizerak the one pool shooter who is recognizable to a wide au-

dience, and so Steve is especially in demand when pool competitions are televised. Minnesota Fats had a widely recognized name, but Fats's countenance was hardly in the public domain. Old-timers like Willie Hoppe and Willie Mosconi had names, but no visibility at all. Thanks to Lite commercials, Steve Mizerak is indisputably the most famous pool shooter of all time. Without exaggeration, Steve says: "That commercial changed my life one hundred percent."

Marv Throneberry of Colliersville, Tennessee, is perhaps the one All-Star who can say his selection is thanks to the old New York bias that once ruled sports commercials but that has been all but free from Lite casting. McCann-Erickson was looking for an athlete who was famous for being bumbling and self-denigrating, the sort of role Joe Garagiola had made a career out of. Throneberry came immediately to mind because he had played for the original "Amazin' Mets" of 1962, the expansion team that lost 120 of 162 games.

Throneberry had become a camp figure, the prime symbol of the team's ineptitude. A first baseman, Throneberry was, in fact, one of the team's better players, but he had an aw-shucks manner, the mistakes he made were never run-of-the-mill, and he got tagged with the unforgettable nickname Marvelous Marv. Soon lost in the miasma of Metsamania was the fact that Throneberry had originally gained his nickname from on high, and for the most sincere of reasons. When he hit a key home run, Mrs. Joan Payson, the team owner, happily exclaimed in her seat: "Isn't that marvelous?" The name stuck, but was twisted with facetiousness.

Notwithstanding, even if the whole world learned how hopeless the Amazin' Mets were, it was not a subject that dented American consciousness much below the level of a Johnny Carson joke. Then, after the 1963 season, Marvelous Marv retired, his fleeting comic fame soon forgotten. And so,

when the commercials started running thirteen years later, a great many viewers were amused, but really didn't appreciate the whole joke. At one point *Sports Illustrated* even felt compelled to write a small item explaining who Marvelous Marv was (had been).

As it was, Throneberry very nearly didn't make the commercial. When Blackman called him up and said he was a New York agent and wanted him to audition for a commercial, Throneberry almost hung up on him, suspicious that the whole thing was a put-on. A few nights before, Rod Kanehl (now we're talking deep trivia), a teammate of Throneberry's on the Mets, had run across some old Mets' fan in a bar somewhere, bet the fellow that he did too know Marvelous Marv, and then called Throneberry collect in Colliersville. Marvelous was not amused on that occasion, and now he figured that Blackman was just another Kanehl telephone prank. Finally Blackman got Throneberry at least to consider that he might be bona fide, and to take down his 212 number so that he could then call Blackman collect.

But two days went by, and no call came from Colliersville. The agency was all over Blackman—what do you mean Marv Throneberry won't call back? It is one thing if Sugar Ray Robinson isn't interested. But Marvelous Marv Throneberry! Finally Marv called, believed Blackman, and agreed to come to New York. At LaGuardia he was met by a limousine. Never having been in one before, he promptly hopped into the front seat next to the driver.

At the time Throneberry was general manager of a small insulating company. Since then he has made eleven more

Lite commercials and is always in demand for personal appearances. He is utterly unpretentious, exactly as he appears on TV, and has the special quality of relating well to the man in the street. Carl Spielvogel believes that Throneberry comes across so well because he possesses a Walter Mitty-like quality. "America can just see what a wonderful, decent human being he is," Bob Meury says. Nice guys finish first.

Whatever he is, Marv is not a man of many demands. When I first met him, before we filmed our commercial with Billy Martin in September 1981, we were at the hotel in New York, waiting to go to a preproduction meeting. Marv noticed I was carrying a garment bag. "What you got there?" he inquired.

I told him that I had been advised to bring some sports coats, one of which might be used for the shoot. "Take 'em back," Marv said. "They're always telling you to bring clothes to these things. But if you don't have what they got in mind, they'll *give* you a good coat to wear. And then, after you've had it on under those lights, they gotta let you keep it."

"Is that so?" I asked.

"Oh, yeah. And a real good coat, too. You know, they must be worth seventy-five dollars."

Armed with this inside scoop, I rushed back to my room and dropped off the sports jacket I thought they were most likely to choose. And sure enough, when I displayed my collection at the production office, the costume people said things like, "Is that all you've got? Oh, that will never do." Marv winked at me.

"Come on over here and let's see what we can put on you," the wardrobe woman said. There were all sorts of jackets there my size. This time, Marv gave me a huge stage wink. They dressed me in a handsome brown Harris tweed, which remains, to this day, the foundation of my winter wardrobe. I never fail to think of Marv whenever I put it on.

As for Marv, he has long since left the insulating company behind and lives happily on what he makes from his Lite appearances and commercials. I do worry about him a little, though. The trouble is that whereas he goes along with the Marvelous Marv gag for the campaign, he has taken to letting interviewers and other well-wishers know that he really wasn't a bum.

There is some truth in that, too. Throneberry's major-league career spanned eleven seasons, and he lost many of his best years because he was caught in the Yankee farm system and had to stay down in the minors. But he did play in one World Series, he hit fifty-three home runs in the majors, and he was often—get this—used as a defensive specialist in the late innings. When he finally was freed from the Yankees, he went to Kansas City in a trade for a guy named Roger Maris, and after his Mets sojourn, he was sold to the Orioles for $125,000—at a time when this was still real money.

I keep telling Marv to keep those facts to himself before he louses up a good thing. So far, though, making a public display of having been a stiff hasn't affected him at all. "My life hasn't changed that much," he says. "The only thing is, I just don't work eight-to-five anymore. But it's the same friends. The same places. The same bars. The only real difference in my life is, I have more time for my huntin' and my fishin'."

*Frank Deford,
Billy Martin,
and Marv
Throneberry*

Nine Lites for Ten Years

One of the hoariest sports trivia questions is the one that goes: Who is the only person to have played for the Dodgers, Knicks, and Rangers?
Answer: Gladys Goodding.

Ms. Goodding played the national anthem and other oldies but goodies on the organ at Madison Square Garden and Ebbets Field.

Next question.

All right, who has appeared in every Lite Beer commercial?

Answer: Eddie Barth.

Next question.

Who is Eddie Barth?

Next answer: Eddie Barth is the announcer, the golden throat who says: "Lite Beer from Miller. Everything you've always wanted in a beer . . . and less."

Barth, from Philadelphia, is fifty-one years old, and has been an actor for twenty-eight years, appearing in a number of TV series and in many films, most recently *Fame*, where he played the cabdriver father. Through the years he has also been the voice for many commercials, the most famous being the Alka-Seltzer campaign, the one that was as much a favorite in its brief heyday as Lite is now. That was the one where there were little vignettes, with tag lines like: "Try it, you'll like it." And: "I can't believe I ate the whole thing." Now you remember. Then Eddie would come on and say, "Alka-Seltzer goes to work . . ." and so on.

When Lite No. 1, the original Matt Snell shoot, was being scheduled, an announcer was needed, and Bob Lenz remembered some of Barth's work. His agent heard from Lenz and called Eddie. Oddly enough, Barth was faced with a choice. Another well-established beer wanted him to do voiceovers for its new national commercials. With residuals, this could mean something like $10,000 or $15,000 for Barth. But, oh yes, the agent went on, there was this other offer. Miller was bringing out some cockamamie diet beer that was going to try to go into test market with a football player. Eddie would be guaranteed nothing but scale: $109. Should I explain to Bob Lenz that you have the other beer?

Barth started to agree. Naturally. Then he paused. "Let me go get a cup of coffee," he said. For reasons he is not really sure of—why did Marv Throneberry call Marty Blackman back? Why did Bob Lenz get on that fateful bus?— Barth came back to his agent's office, and this is what he said: "Go with the Miller."

In the decade since that magic moment, Barth has been Lite's only voice. For radio commercials,☆ he must do new work every time one is recorded, for unlike TV, where graphics identify the characters—RODNEY DANGERFIELD Famous Swinger, BOB UECKER Mr. Baseball, etc.—Garth must provide this identification orally over the radio. For TV he has long since recorded the tag line in bulk: a little bit fast, a little bit slow, louder, softer, with all sorts of varying speeds and inflections, and so depending on exactly how long (to the split second) the commercial runs and the nature of the bit, the exactly correct "Lite Beer from Miller. Everything you always wanted in a beer . . . and less" may be dropped in.

Occasionally though, Barth is flown to New York for special voiceovers. For example, for Lite No. 31, in December 1977, the one in which Boom-Boom Geoffrion and Jacques Plante have a LF/TG argument in French, Barth, who comes "from a family of screaming Italians" and knows no French whatsoever, was brought in to record the usual ender in French; the words were written out for him phonetically. For the recent softball Alumni commercial, he had to re-

☆ In relation to traditional beers, Lite uses little radio advertising. Radio, at least for beers, is presumed to reach a younger audience, and the light beer drinker's profile is inclined more toward middle age.

EDDIE BARTH

cord an unusual highly excited tag line, inasmuch as it would come right after the Doll stroked the winning home run. "I just gave it my best Marty Glickman," Eddie says.

On another occasion Eddie was brought to New York in the hopes that a voiceover could save a commercial. ☆

In the fall of 1982, Butkus and Nitschke were joined by three other erstwhile linebackers, Tommy Nobis, Bill Bergey, and Willie Lanier. The idea was that it would be a bunch of tough guys acting tough, until, at the very end, they would reveal their true colors by waving and saying "Hi, Mom!" to the camera.

Unfortunately, even with the sweet closer, the linebackers never seemed anything but mean and intimidating—very definitely, one of the agency guys says, "not the sort of people you would want to have a beer with." And that, after all, is the idea. Still, there remained hope that somehow the commercial could be salvaged, and so Eddie Barth was called in to record a new tag line. He would say: "Lite Beer from Miller. Everything you always wanted in a beer . . . and less." And then Eddie would cry out, "Hi, Mom!"

Cute idea. Still couldn't save the commercial.

What Barth has been saying at the end of commercials for ten years now is all the more important because it is crucial to the brewery that the specific phrase "Lite Beer From Miller" be established in the public mind. Most people, of course, do not step up to the bar and say, "Gimme a Lite Beer From Miller." Instead, they say, "Gimme a Lite." Maybe they say, "Gimme a Miller Lite"— which is, in fact, how Spillane referred to the beer for many of the takes in Lite No. 2. But finally it was decided to stick with "Lite Beer From Miller."

Miller decided to stay with the wordier version for two reasons. First, there is a great similarity between *Lite* and High *Life*—and Miller High Life was already well established. Second, and especially in the beginning, before the U. S. Supreme Court refused to consider such a trademark claim, Miller was hoping that the specific and repeated use of Lite as a brand name would enjoin other brewers from using "light" in their brands.

As it turned out, Lite was the victim of its own success. The brand was so well received so quickly that "light" became accepted as a generic term for all such beers. The Supreme Court just wasn't going to get into that. It had other fish to fry.

An even better idea would be to get the Supreme Court to make it unlawful for anybody to say "a third less calories than their regular beer." Nobody who

☆ Through the years, five Lite commercials have been auditioned, approved, shot, edited to the correct length, and then junked, never to be shown on the air.

speaks English would ever say such a thing. They would say: "Lite has a third less calories than *your* regular beer." Wouldn't they? But that wasn't permitted, because how could you then prove that Lite had a third less than Brand X or Brand Y?

So why not say: "Lite has a third less calories than *our* regular beer." That, after all, is what it says on a can or bottle of Lite. Pick it up. Look at it: "our regular beer." See.

But the agency didn't want Lite celebrities saying that and giving the impression they worked for all the Miller beers. No, they were just Lite folks. So, "our" was out too. That is when it was decided that everybody would say, "Lite has a third less calories than *their* regular beer." That made everybody happy, even though it sounds like somebody from Uruguay wrote it.

It is also true—as the agency later found out—that "a third less calories" is incorrect. It should be, "a third fewer calories." But . . . "The word *fewer* just doesn't come out of a man's mouth," Bob Meury explains.

Next question.

Whatever happened to Eddie Barth?

Well, not long ago someone at Backer & Spielvogel came up with the idea that they should write a Lite commercial starring Eddie's face as well as his voice. An audition tape was made, too, but Miller wouldn't go for it. They thought it was just a third more inside than their regular commercials. So the commercial was never shot.

But at least Eddie is still the answer to that trivia question: Who has appeared in every Lite commercial?

Answer: No one.

In Lite No. 12, starring Rosie Grier and Friends, the tag line was done in needlepoint, not spoken. And in Lite No. 69, the Christmas commercial, there is no tag line at all.

Eddie Barth. Everything you always wanted in a commercial . . . except two.

LEFT TO RIGHT:
Ben Davidson,
Rosie Grier,
and Ray Nitschke

Ten Quarts

When the All-Stars are thrown together to make their annual group commercial, there is a predictable amount of clowning around between shots.

In one slow moment, Martin dresses up in catcher's gear, puts on some makeup and a bandanna round his head, and goes over and bows to Numa like a Samurai—with lots of "ah sos," too. Bubba leans down and talks into Lee's cleavage. Deacon groggily climbs onto the team bus at 7:30 a.m., unsuspecting, thinking he's only going off to location. But unbeknowst to him, buried deep inside the business section of this morning's newspaper, someone has come across a tiny item about a limousine company that Deacon owns being involved in a minor financial dispute. "Deacon's my name, Nonpayment's my game," some All-Star hoots, parodying Deacon's commercial bit, and soon there is no mercy for him at all. In the midst of a posed group portrait, Madden reaches down and pinches Lee on her rear end. Lee swiftly jerks her head around to catch the culprit. Too late. Madden is already looking away, innocently studying the horizon. This is a grown man with a son in college. But who is directly behind Lee and the obvious perpetrator? Heinsohn. She glares at him. For once Heinsohn is speechless. To protest in any way, he knows, would only certify his apparent guilt all the more.

From the first day I became involved with the All-Stars, everybody kept telling me how much I was going to love seeing the outtakes of old commercials. Outtakes are film that wasn't used on the air. Boy, was I going to love the outtakes. Everybody thought the outtakes that had been saved were the funniest things they had ever seen. I finally saw a reel of the best outtakes. Mostly it was just guys missing their lines, or Bubba hitting his head on the door and then saying a dirty word. But the All-Stars love the outtakes and love hearing one another say real dirty words on film.

When the cameras are not rolling, there is, as you might expect, the usual sort of men-in-groups banter about women, money, and other semi-essentials of middle age—lies and stories. An ugly conversation comes up. All-Ugly teams are always a divertissement with athletes. One All-Star remembers a coach so ugly that the only girl he ever picked up turned out to be a transvestite. Heinsohn suggests a former seven-foot center as the ugliest player he ever saw. The guy was white. There is a certain amount of tact, even in ugly discussions: the white guys stick pretty much to nominating ugly whites, the blacks ugly blacks. Bubba has a black candidate, an old offensive lineman who bit Bubba once. "This guy was so ugly, you could tell he was ugly from the back," Bubba explains.

Among the group, by far the most badinage is directed at Bubba. He is especially fair game because he misses his lines the most. In one Alumni commercial, Rodney said: "Is everybody here?" Bubba was supposed to reply: "Yah, everybody who *is* somebody"—emphasis on the *is*. But he kept putting it on the *some*. They made up cue cards with *IS* underlined and capitalized. It still took him forever to get that straight, and of course, the All-Stars never let him forget it until the next gaffe.

Perhaps his most famous one was when his line—remem-

ber?—was simply: "Says here the winner is . . . Bubba Smith." Only one time Bubba said, "Says here the winner is . . ." and he forgot his name.

At Feibel's Bowling Alley in Teaneck, New Jersey, where the bowling commercial was being shot, Bubba was supposed to break holes in a fake bowling ball right after Butkus handed it to him and said: "Hey, Bubba, this ball doesn't have any holes in it."

"It does now," Bubba said, as he broke through.

One time, though, a real hole-less ball was substituted, and the others, like little kids in on a joke, could hardly keep from laughing even before Bubba did a double-take and tried to break through. Later, no matter how many times he said, "It does now," they would all—black and white—scream, "It do now" at it. He never once said that.

Actually, the best faux pas Bubba really did make was in Lite No. 65, when he and Butkus were "us linksters" on the course. All sorts of different endings were tried, and the commercial required something like sixty-five takes. But one line pretty much stayed throughout. That was Bubba saying, "Yeah, it's a lot easier hitting a quarterback than a little white ball." Only one time Bubba said, "Yeah, it's a lot easier hitting a little white quarterback."

On another occasion Bubba got the last word in. He was, along with Deacon, going in to be made up for one of the Alumni commercials. As two of them came into the dressing room, the little makeup man—an Oriental fellow who also happened to be terribly effeminate—blanched at these two huge black behemoths coming at him. In his day-to-day work with actors, nothing had prepared him for this, and, discombobulated, he gasped, "I won't do black guys."

Apparently, what he meant was that he didn't have the right sort of cosmetics to use on black skins at this moment, but Bubba and Deacon didn't wait for an amplification. They picked up the poor little fellow and started to hand him out the window.

They were thirty-five floors up.

Thereafter, the little guy never left the Doll's side.

Actually, Bubba is one of the better-acting All-Stars, and like a number of them he makes at least a portion of his living as an actor. For a long time Bubba was a regular on a TV show entitled *Open All Night,* and this past summer he could be seen with Burt Reynolds, playing a chauffeur in a movie called *Stroker Ace.*

Deacon Jones—square name: David—who played in the NFL for fourteen years, ten as an All-Pro, and will forever be remembered as the man who coined the work "sack," had his own nightclub act for a while, singing and dancing, and threatening to become a male stripper. ("Wouldn't you buy a ticket to see this body naked?") He has appeared on several TV shows and in movies as well, highlighted by an appearance in *The Norseman,* an epic in which Deacon claims to have played "the only black Viking in history." Carlos Palomino has appeared in *Taxi,* and while Happy Hairston is now on the other side of the 10 percent, serving as an agent for athletes, for a time he was himself a Hollywood actor. Ben Davidson appeared in the movie of *M*A*S*H,* as well as a number of TV series, such as *Fantasy Island* and *Happy Days.* Other athletes who appeared in past Lite commercials and have also acted include Rosie Grier and Fred "The Hammer" Williamson.

There is some correlation between the All-Stars who are the finest actors and those who made the most appearances. For that matter, a high percentage of jocks who audition are rejected. By the time Giraldi or some other director gets an athlete before live cameras he is not just working with nothing. He has the *crème de la crème.* All-Stars improve with work, too. In the beginning Billy Martin had a reputation as a woeful performer and temperamental to boot, but after all his commercials for Lite, as well as for a pipe tobacco, a bank, carpets, Pepto-Bismol, and Billyball itself, Martin is now accomplished enough. In the commercial he did with

Throneberry and me, Martin didn't have any lines—just facial expressions—and Jeff Lovinger, the director, had to keep toning Martin down from *over*acting. It was sort of the Billy Martin Method School. Today, Martin admits, he'd like very much to cap his acting career with a substantial part in a cowboy movie.

Already past the scheming stage is a movie that would involve a couple of dozen or more All-Stars. The producer is Don Ohlmeyer, formerly the chief of NBC Sports, now an independent producer. The plot centers on a character (to be played by Marvelous Marv) who invents a process whereby water can be turned into gas. As they say in Century City, it's going through rewrites.

There is a camaraderie that can be sensed when the All-Stars get together—that is for real. Madden says—and very earnestly: "What I like about this is how you become a part of something. And that's the one thing we all understand, and I think it's great."

But keep in mind, as with any team, there are vast differences in cultural background and personality that separate the various All-Stars. And of course, unlike other teammates, they are not bound by a common game. Grits Gresham—Charles Hamilton, Jr.—is shooting editor of *Sports Afield* magazine and has written five books: he has a master's degree in wildlife management. (He was also, as was Don Carter, a failed minor-league baseball aspirant.) Buck Buchanan is a strong, silent type who runs a nightclub in Kansas City, Missouri. Bruce Wilhelm is the only one of the lot to have won an Olympic medal (a bronze in 1976, for weightlifting), but he, like Mizerak, spent many years as a high school teacher. Dick Williams has spent virtually all of his last thirty-five years in the major leagues all over—as a player with Brooklyn, Baltimore, Cleveland, Kansas City, and Boston, and as a manager with Boston, Oakland, California, Montreal, and San Diego. Rodney Marsh first came to America from England in 1976. Bob Uecker regularly plays the *To-*

night Show. Jim Shoulders raises rodeo stock and runs a rodeo training school. Carlos Palomino came from Tijuana, Mexico, and is the only boxer ever to win a world title and graduate from college (Long Beach State) in the same year. Boog Powell "majored in curve balls" and runs a marina. And so on.

As disparate as they are, when the All-Stars do get together, they tend to separate naturally by age and sport. Generally, the guys from the main American team sports—baseball, football, and basketball—tend to congregate. Over here, for example, is Madden, doing a takeoff of baseball managers giving signs, for the amusement of Williams and Martin. A lot of the All-Stars may accurately be described as overweight, but only Mizerak, the pool player, tends to get kidded about that. Not the fat old heroes from the real sports.

Actually, one of the worst natural athletes in the group is one of the biggest and strongest—Ben Davidson from football. When he first threw a softball around, getting ready for a commercial, people thought he was imitating the Doll. "Throw it for real next time," someone said. Only that *was* for real. Later, shagging flies in right field, with the *Los Angeles Times* editorial page sticking out his back pocket be-

tween pitches, Davidson stumbled back on a long fly, caught it while falling backward, hit the prop fence, knocked it and fell flat out on his back. But he did hang onto the ball.

Then he lobbed it back into the infield like a girl.

Indeed, underneath his huge frame and the wonderful rich voice that goes with it, Davidson is one of the more reflective and sensitive of the All-Stars. "I'm just the big guy in the back row," he says. When he was first presented with the script for Lite No. 72, in which he whips another guy in the bar at arm wrestling, he resisted the idea. "I was obviously going to be bigger than the fellow I was paired against," Ben says. "How could I possibly smirk at him, the way I was supposed to, after I beat him? But I finally realized it was just another cartoon, and people would accept it if I played it that way."

Madden, who was Davidson's coach with the Raiders, says, "Ben really didn't like sports. He liked motorcycles and weird stuff like that."

Madden himself comes in for an extra amount of teasing because of his phobia of flying. Despite his florid, happy-go-lucky air—for a long time his friends called him "Pinky"—Madden was driven from coaching (as was Geoffrion) by ul-

CLOCKWISE FROM LOWER LEFT: *Steve Mizerak, Grits Gresham, Jim Honochick, Bubba Smith, Boog Powell, Carlos Palomino, Billy Martin, Dick Butkus, Tommy Heinsohn, John Madden, and Marv Throneberry*

cers, and despite his heavy travel schedule—especially in the autumn, when he is CBS's top football commentator—Madden journeys only by Amtrak. He finds it very soothing. "I was really influenced by *Travels With Charley*," he says, "and I always wanted to take a trip like that myself. Well, traveling by train is like *Charley*. The only difference is, on the train, America gets on and travels with you from town to town, then it gets off."

At the Christmas commercial shoot two years ago, Madden was the one who took most of the kidding. The other All-Stars thought that Miller, as a public service, should relinquish some of the thirty seconds in order for Madden to wish his family—the one he never sees because he's on trains all the time—a Merry Christmas.

Boog Powell is another one of the All-Stars who comes in for a lot of friendly kidding, especially since Giraldi tends to get on his case all the time. It is revealing that Boog is the only All-Star who has worked two continuing shticks with two different All-Stars—the blind umpire and the Japanese ballplayer. As much as anything, this is testament to the fact that Boog comes across on the screen for exactly what he is, genuine and friendly, good company for anyone, one of nature's noblemen. One day last spring I was talking to Jim Kern, who has pitched for four major-league teams in the last decade. Kern started naming the "best people" he had ever met in baseball over all those years. He settled on five names. Four of them, like Kern, were pitchers. The fifth was Boog Powell.

But the other All-Stars, in typical team fashion, will start to razz Boog as soon as they see that Coach Giraldi has him heated up. At the bowling commercial last year, the first day's shooting was running long. Among other things, that morning, just when they were turning on the smoke machines in order to give the place its properly hazy look, a real electrical fire broke out and everybody had to be herded out into the brisk December chill; a whole hour or so was

Boog Powell

lost before Giraldi and his charges were allowed back before the cameras.

Then Boog couldn't get it right. At least Giraldi said he couldn't. This was the bit when Boog has to rush up and stop Honochick from bowling in the wrong direction. And everybody was involved—both the Less Fillings and the Taste Greats had to stand there. And Boog just couldn't get it. "Be bigger! Be bigger!" Giraldi screamed, as if he were dealing with Sir Laurence Olivier. What the hell is "be bigger?" Boog Powell *bigger?* "Do it from here!" Butkus called out, imitating Giraldi, and the others all joined in, most particularly Bubba, who was delighted that it was somebody else who was taking all the heat. He screamed out one more final dig at Boog.

That did it. Boog, beet-red now, really hot under the collar, turned around and glared at Bubba. "Watch it," he said. Then he waved a finger. I started looking around for the exit sign. If this went on any further, there goes the bowling alley: Boog and Bubba would be like bull elephants trampling down the veld. But it lasted only a moment. Bubba understood things had gone too far. He nodded, nicely. Boog turned around, went back to acting, got bigger, and gave Giraldi the take he wanted.

We Need Eleven Over Here

Once the cameras start grinding, the All-Stars become very professional. Occasionally, one or two will admit that a commercial goes better after a lunch break when they can sample some of the product and loosen up, but usually it's all business. Bob Uecker recalls that when his first commercial was dragging on, he suggested to Giraldi that they take a break and quaff a couple quickies, but Giraldi snapped at him like a Dutch uncle to behave himself.

What hijinks there are usually take place only near the end of the shoot, when the director is just making a few more takes for protection, to keep the client happy. At that point, for example, someone stiffed Heinsohn with a real jalapeño pepper, instead of a candy prop. Davidson and the actor he was arm wrestling with staged a mock fight after one late take that really did fool everybody. The opponent acted as if he was tired of always getting whipped and jumped Davidson. They knocked over chairs and tables, frightened the crew, until they let on that it was all a gag.

In all the commercials, the participant most seriously injured was Koichi Numazawa, in his first effort with Boog Powell. Numa, a former catcher in the Japanese leagues, is now a broadcast commentator and newspaper columnist in Tokyo. Numa had met Powell when the Orioles toured Japan

Koichi Numazawa

one autumn, but Boog didn't remember the little fellow, and so here he was, his first trip to the States, alone with only an interpreter, asked to bash a table in two—something nothing in his life had prepared him for. And Giraldi was the director—Giraldi, who often says, "That's excellent, but you can do better." Imagine getting that through translation.

Giraldi wanted to make sure that there was no visible crease where the table was split. The crack was covered by a tablecloth, the two halves held together with thin pieces of balsa wood. Unfortunately, the table turned out to be more difficult to break than it was supposed to be, and after a while Numa's hand started swelling up. "Numa was really hot for a while," Boog says. "If it had been me, if they'd hauled me across the ocean, and kept making me hurt my hand, I'd have finally said, 'Enough of this crap.' " As it was, Giraldi finally relented, getting one of his finest commercials after sixteen takes.

And the next time Numa crossed the Pacific, to bust up the table in the Friday Night Card Game skit, everybody made sure that the table split apart much easier.

It is not at all unusual for different endings to be shot, or for new punch lines to be adlibbed on the spot. Especially by now, when so many of the Lite characters are well established, once a situation is set up, alternative dialogue can flow out of it naturally. The characters have, in a sense, taken precedence over the routines. Bob Lenz says, "Lite is probably the first time that a commercial campaign has played off past commercials in the campaign—although, of course, each commercial has to stand on its own as well."

One of the most popular of all Lite commercials was the one with Jim Shoulders, which ends with Billy Martin turning around and saying, "I didn't punch that doggie." That commercial went through a multitude of transmutations, starting with an original idea that Shoulders would be the only All-Star featured, but that some actor playing a tenderfoot—perhaps with an English accent—would close it by saying something like, "Why would anyone want to punch a little doggie?" But eventually Martin was included in the script with Shoulders, and another half-dozen or more variations on the theme were suggested.

Bob Meury was overseeing the commercial, but he wasn't directly involved in it. He loved the idea, but he thought it just missed. On the day of the shoot, which took place in a bar in downtown Manhattan, when Meury found he had some spare time, he popped into Lenz's office, and they decided to run down and watch the commercial being made for a little while. It was while Meury was standing there watching Martin and Shoulders do a take of the final script that he got his inspiration.

Meury went over to Giraldi and whispered in his ear: "Why don't you try this, Billy saying: 'I didn't punch that doggie'?" Giraldi roared, pulled Martin aside, and gave him the new punch line; when they went before the cameras again there weren't but a handful of people in the room—just a few out of maybe thirty-five or forty—who knew what was coming.

Jim Shoulders and Billy Martin

The place completely broke up when Martin spoke the new gag. The rest was easy.

"I went right out and got a cab back to the office," Meury says. "Quit while you're ahead."

When I did the commercial with Billy and Marv, the original punch line had Marv saying: "I don't know why they wanted Billy Martin to do this commercial." On paper that was the funnier line; I still think it's the funnier line. It played off Marv's old, most familiar line. But after about twenty takes, when we had that version safely done, Nick Gisonde decided to try the alternative ending that had been discussed, Marv and I clinking glasses, and Marv saying: "Cheer up, Billy, someday you'll be famous just like me." It was almost an afterthought; we only did five takes of that. But that, of course, was the one selected.

Backer & Spielvogel has discussed the possibility of someday using two versions of a commercial. That is, one version would be shown for the first few weeks, and then, just as everybody in America knew the gag word for word and was speaking the dialogue in chorus, the agency would slip in the commercial with a different punch line. That would be another first for Lite.

The All-Stars themselves always exhibit a certain residual competitiveness. How do you compete in acting? Well, for the veteran All-Stars, the big statistic is the Number of Takes required for them to do a commercial. You can almost visualize one of them going in to see Marty Blackman and demanding a raise for next year because he had good Takes stats. The All-Stars are forever comparing Takes. "How many Takes did you need?" "I only took twenty-six Takes." And so on.

It is well documented that the record for most Takes is held by Steve Mizerak: 181. Now, understand, this involved making a very difficult trick pool shot. It wasn't that it took Steve 181 takes just to say correctly: "Lite has a third less calories than their regular beer." Still, he had heard so much razzing over the years about his 181 Takes, that by now Steve gets very testy whenever the subject comes up. "Listen, we had that commercial after sixty Takes," he says stoutly. "We did it right again after seventy-five. They just kept on because they wanted to make *sure* we had it."

But the saddest I ever saw any All-Star was Bob Uecker. This is the Life Imitates Art department. It was during the

Bob Uecker

filming of the softball commercial, and here was the situation: The Doll is standing up, on deck. She sort of jiggles in place (Lee can do this), while cooing, "My turn, my turn!" Frank Robinson, manager of the Tastes Greats, asks if there are any pinch hitters left who can swing for Lee. At this point, the script calls for Uecker to raise his hand and say, "Yeah." Then, of course, all the other TGs moan, so Lee gets a chance to swing for herself.

After a few takes (excellent, but could be better), Giraldi suggested that Uecker try saying something besides just plain "Yeah." Uecker, elated at this expression of confidence in his dramatic abilities, worked up a number of variations, e.g., "Send me in," "I can do it," "Give me a chance, Skip." That kind of stuff. All demonstrably better lines than "Yeah."

Giraldi thought it over after taping several of these alternatives. "No," he said at last. "Just do the 'Yeah,' Bob. Go back to the 'Yeah.'"

Uecker was crestfallen. Here is a guy who makes a good living putting himself down. The bit before the camera at this very moment was an A-1 putdown. But now he had genuinely struck out. He had been dropped in the order, cut down, waived, optioned, released. His jaw fell slack; his face dropped. It was several more takes before Uecker got off another good "Yeah."

The next day all the Tastes Greats (Uecker excepted) were called for batting practice. Giraldi wanted some simple stock shots of each of them hitting. Dick Williams was pitching. "Low ball hitter, highball drinker," Williams screamed. He was just lobbing them in there, because all Giraldi wanted was for each Tastes Great to take a nice level swing, meet the ball, drive a liner back up the middle, and then take about three steps toward first as if he were running out a hit. Got it? Easy swing, hit a drive up the middle, start to run to first. Simple. Yes?

No.

Because the minute the All-Stars found themselves in the batter's box, every one of them was an athlete again, on trial, competing. Each one suddenly wanted to pull home runs. Bubba swung so hard he missed completely. "Don't worry, Bubba," Williams said, preparing to lob another lollypop, "it took Lee a while too." Even Frank Robinson got caught up in the competition. Now really, F. Robby hardly had anything to prove. He had hit merely 586 *real* home runs in the majors. But even he started swinging from the heels. He tried so hard on one pitch, he barely touched it and dribbled it back to the mound. "Well, I don't feel so bad now," Bubba said.

Moreover, to Giraldi's growing consternation, the All-Stars got so wrapped up in slugging for the fences that no matter where they hit a pitch—even if they hit a beautiful line drive up the middle, which was the idea—they'd forget to drop their bat and dig for first, but instead would just stand at the plate and admire their handiwork. It took forever to get the simple stock shots. The old juices were really flowing again.

Interestingly, when shooting commercials Lite takes its All-Stars first class in every instance but one. Everything is top rank—airplanes, limousines, hotels, all the amenities— except when the boys go to shoot an Alumni commercial. Then, just like a team, they depart by bus. It leaves the hotel at some ungodly early hour, and everybody better be there.

Rodney, however, doesn't ride the team bus. He shows up later in the day, only when he is needed. Unlike the sports stars, Mickey and the Doll, all the famous Lite heroes, Rodney is not officially an All-Star. ☆ His trademark white shirt and red tie may have been on display at the Smithsonian, he is one of the most famous comedians in the country, his "I don't get no respect" is a part of the culture, but Rodney is never really a part of the All-Stars, a member of the *team*.

☆ Numa is the other exception; Miller sells no beer in Japan.

Maybe all the athletes intimidate him in some way. After all, his act is not just an act; as Giraldi says, "Rodney's insecurity is unbelievable."

Actually, the All-Stars don't really know Rodney; he keeps too much distance. It is only because of his special treatment that he suffers constant heckling and backbiting from them. Since Numa joined the troupe, everybody calls Dangerfield "Lodney," as Numa does. Typical of the way the All-Stars respond to Rodney was when he showed up at the softball shoot this past year, hours after the others had come in the bus, all the guys assembled as a group. Then, led by Martin, as soon as Lodney made his entrance, they all screamed, in chorus, "big deal" (only there was another word between the big and the deal). You can get away with any number of things when you're on a team. You can be outgoing, private, noisy, quiet, profane, religious. About the only one thing you can't be is a big deal.

But perhaps Rodney is feeling more team-y at last. For the last four years, the Alumni commercial festivities have included a team banquet, and this past year, at the Beverly Hills Hotel, Rodney was in attendance for the whole evening, for the first time. Bob Uecker was the featured after-dinner speaker, doing his routine, which is, essentially, Rodney Dangerfield Goes to the National League. Uecker jokes are Rodney jokes, same root. Uecker brought the house down, too. He was in peak form.

Then Rodney was invited up to the mike, and he graciously and very professionally followed Uecker's tough act by telling only a couple of special Lite jokes—no more. "I started drinking Lite Beer, and since then I've gained sixteen pounds." And to Geoffrion, in the audience: "Hey, Boom-Boom, I know your sister, Bang-Bang." It was a start.

Two Six-Packs

The idea for a Lite commercial develops in many ways. One way it does not come about, however, is for somebody to phone or write Backer & Spielvogel with a suggestion. John Griswold, a Yalie, is the account director, a Backer vice-president, and all unsolicited mail about the campaign ends up on his desk. The instant he starts to read a letter and suspects that a suggestion is coming, he stops reading, hands the letter over to his secretary, and has it returned along with a standard note, explaining that no outside suggestions can be considered. The campaign is also so well known that regularly, as well, Griswold has friends and associates who call up, and say, "John,

I've got a great idea for a new Lite commercial. Bubba and Butkus are in diving helmets at the Indy 500, when—"

Stop! says John Griswold. Don't tell me any more. "I'm sure we miss out on some terrific ideas," he explains. "But the problem is, that if we started considering suggestions we would end up rejecting most, and then, months later, if we did a commercial that in any way resembled an idea somebody had sent in, we'd be sued for stealing their original concept."

As you know, Shakespeare borrowed most of his plots. There just aren't that many simple schemes you can work into less than thirty seconds. As it is, even Lite has borrowed some. Buck Buchanan's "The buck stops here," was, of course, first made famous by a sign on Harry Truman's desk. Bubba Smith quoted Humphrey Bogart in one commercial ("Tennis anyone?" was a line Bogie originally uttered in a Broadway play) and Big Daddy Lipscomb in another. Big Daddy, ex-Colt, ex-Steeler, really is supposed to have said: "I just grab each guy who comes through and throw them away one by one till I find the one with the ball"—which is approximately what Bubba says in Lite No. 25.

In any event, by the time a commercial is aired, its authorship may well be in doubt. One writer may have come up with the concept, while another wrote the bulk of the script, and then somebody else suggested a better ending. It is generally a group exercise, and of the many writers at Backer who try Lite scripts, most work in teams. From the very beginning, Lite has been known as "a writer's account," and for script meetings everybody is anxious to pitch in and try one, even if Lite is not their regular account. Charlie Breen, currently the head writer for Lite, says, "More people are involved all the time, for the simple reason that it gets harder since so many good ideas have already been taken." Nobody keeps any figures, but it is estimated that for every twenty Lite scripts that are submitted in the roughest early form, only three or four ever are accepted merely as feasible possibilities. And that's just the start of the winnowing process.

Some scripts read well, but (it becomes obvious) just can't play well. Some the agency adores, but Miller doesn't like. "It's a tough account," Lenz says. "Miller probably rejects some of the best commercials in the industry." It isn't scientific. Some people were flabbergasted when Miller decided to go with a bullfight spot, while it has rejected commercials that seemed bland in New York.

And then, a special problem arises when a new All-Star is called for. In the eighty-one Lite commercials aired in the first ten years, seventy-four different featured players have been used. This goes through cycles, but, generally speaking, fewer newcomers have been used lately. In fact, it wasn't until Lite No. 69, late in 1981, that the number of commercials aired outnumbered the number of characters used in the commercials.

And finding the right types is not all that easy. Lenz never forgets being touted on Red Holtzman, then the coach of the Knicks, and certainly one of the least expressive men ever put on God's green earth. They had a portable camera there to record the irrepressible Knick mentor. "Smile," said the cameraman.

"I don't smile," said Holtzman.

Some freeze up before the audition cameras. Others can't be understood. Others, like the scripts, look better on paper. Some guys simply get unlucky: they're fine, but the script fails them. Originally, for example, Lite No. 50 starred three managers giving signs at the bar: Herzog and Williams and Sparky Anderson. But it was too unwieldy with three, and Anderson had to go. (Williams and Herzog were probably a little bit better together because there was genuine bar rapport between them; as journeymen outfielders, they had shared many beers together while playing at Baltimore and Kansas City.) Gail Goodrich tested beautifully in a script about male athletes with girls' names, but the bit just didn't work, and nobody has ever figured out exactly how to spot Goodrich since then.

Some athletes turn Miller down—although not so many in recent years, since the commercials have become a phenomenon. Others may be leery of endorsing an alcoholic beverage. "I drink," Jim Shoulders says. "I drink in front of my kids and I drink in front of my preacher. Still—" When he was first contacted he had reservations about what the identification with a beer would do to his wholesome cowboy image. But it just so happened that Wilt Chamberlain's Lite commercial No. 17 was running at the time, and while Shoulders had never met Wilt, he figured if a big man like that could poke fun at himself, then he should take his own concerns about Jim Shoulders less seriously. And thus did a rodeo star, previously unidentifiable outside of Oklahoma and maybe Wyoming, get "ten thousand Skycaps all over the country suddenly saying 'I didn't punch that doggie' wherever I go."

There are a couple of other prohibitions that can apply too. There is an FCC regulation that anybody who endorses a product on television must aver that he does indeed use it. Likewise, for beer endorsements, you cannot own any share in a saloon or package-goods store. And, of course, an athlete must be retired from his sport—unless, perhaps, he shoots pool or bowls. When the Quarry brothers, Jerry and Mike, arrived in New York in November 1979 for Lite No. 49, Jerry was as flabbergasted as everyone else to learn that his younger brother had just decided to resume his lackluster ring career and had signed for another bout. There went a payday for Jerry—and one of the first he would ever enjoy without bloodying his nose. While the agency people studiously stayed out of this family affair, Jerry—riding with Mike in the backseat of a limousine—convinced his younger brother that they had much more of a future in commercials than in the ring.

It is also the policy in the United States that beer (or wine) cannot be consumed on television in commercials that urge you to drink these products. Of course, actors in dramatic shows can drink all the beer possible on the screen; they can drink grain alcohol on TV; they can drink hemlock. But beer cannot be drunk in beer commercials.

Nowadays, when the Alumni commercials are shot, they are a media event, and TV crews cover the shoot. Thus, sometimes we have had the ludicrous situation in which the television viewer sees ex-athletes drinking beer while making a beer commercial, although they cannot be seen drinking beer on the commercial they are making.

As a consequence of this bizarre policy, the heads on beer become all the more important for TV commercials. If beer can't be drunk, then watching it foam is the closest thing to action. Of course, as you know, anybody who ever drinks beer tries to pour it down the side of the glass precisely so it won't foam up and tickle your nose when you are drinking. But commercials for beer are 180 degrees the other way; foam is sacred. One prop man even has an eggbeater; it is his job to foam up the visible beers all the time.

So, the quest goes on: find the right script, work on it, get it right, then find the right ex-jock to play it. Back in 1980, Doreen Fox, who is in the art department at Backer, worked up a script with Dean Weller, a copywriter. Everybody on the account liked the script. It called for Grits Gresham, the old tall-taler of fish, to swap lies with a lumberjack. It had to be lumberjack because the punch line was that old gag about the Sahara Forest. A very old lumberjack joke, but fun. And a good spot for Grits, too.

And so the call went out from Backer & Spielvogel: get us a lumberjack for this commercial.

Eric Steinhauser, a producer of Lite commercials at Backer, was put in charge of the project. It would go on for more than two years. Carrying a portable camera and a crew around, Eric searched the land, high and low, far and wide, for lumberjacks. He went to lumberjack festivals. He taped almost two hundred possibilities, tested as many as fifty at some length. Alas, lumberjacks are not bred for commercials. Eric says, "You can find baseball players who can talk. You can find football players who can talk. You can even find hockey players who can talk. But you cannot find lumberjacks who can talk. You know, their whole life has been spent out in the woods with dinosaurs."

One lumberjack drove two hours for his audition. The lights went on, and he blacked out at the bar. Keeled right over. Out cold. Eric talked to another perfect candidate on the phone. The guy was articulate and had the right kind of rugged lumberjack voice. Eric drove to meet him. He turned out to be a five-foot-one-inch lumberjack. Another nominee was a man mountain, but he had a voice even squeakier than Jack Nicklaus's. Backer began to drop its strict requirements. A part-time lumberjack would be all right. Still, no luck.

Of course, sometimes it is the opposite, and the casting works out beautifully, right away. A lumberjack they couldn't find, but Grits Gresham was the first fisherman they contacted. Butkus, remember, was the first of the tough linebackers to audition. Boom-Boom was the only real choice for a mean hockey player, and he was a natural, plus French-Canadian, which made him even more ideal, a better stereotype. When big black guys were being tested for the "easy-opening can" spot, Blackman offered three candidates: Bubba, Deacon, and Buck. Bubba was obviously born for the part, but the other two both tested so well that two other commercials were written specifically for them.

Brian Anderson and Grits Gresham

And, even a blind pig finds an acorn now and then. Eric Steinhauser got a tip on a lumberjack up in northwestern Connecticut named Brian Anderson. To be sure: *Connecticut.* This doesn't exactly sound like lumberjack country, not hardly like Oregon or Montana, tree places like that. Still, no longer could the agency be choosy. Steinhauser went to a lumberjack show just to meet Anderson who, it turned out, had gone bluefishing that weekend. Finally Steinhauser ran his quarry down, and was delighted to discover that he had all the ingredients. He was husky and bearded, a nice-looking man of thirty-seven, with a wife and two small sons. On top of everything else, he had been drinking Lite beer for years, even back when it was considered sissy. "Oh, is that you, Brian?" the bartender cooed, throwing a limp wrist at Brian the first time he ordered it. "Mmmm."

Brian also had some show biz coursing in his veins. Part of his business—he cuts mostly red and white oak and ash—consists of going about and drumming up business. Trees don't come to you. On these occasions, Brian would always make sure not to wear city clothes, but to get all decked out in a real stereotyped lumberjack outfit; jeans and checked shirt, big boots and red suspenders that said TIMBER on them. "People don't want to hire a guy in a fancy suit to cut their timber," he explains.

So Brian auditioned, and two hundred or so lumberjacks later, Backer & Spielvogel had their man.

Grits was called. A bar was found. Lite always uses real bars, never sets. Everybody had figured they would have to travel far out of New York City to find a properly woodsy saloon, but somebody came across a nautical place named the New York Boatyard, way up on the East Side. The signs were strictly briny: TO LIFE BOATS (rest rooms in that direction), WE RUN A TIGHT SHIP, CAPTAIN'S QUARTERS, and what have you, but these and other ocean-going accoutrements could be shot around, so long as the big sailfish over the bar could be furloughed for the day. It was taken down and a large big-toothed saw went up in its stead. With the saw in place, with the principals and extras all decked out in appropriate outdoor wear, the New York Boatyard would look as foresty as anything Hansel and Gretel ever wandered into.

Bob Giraldi rounded up his production crew, and early on the morning of November 17, 1981, they assembled at the New York Boatyard, which had been rented for the day, ready to begin to shoot what would be the platinum Lite Beer commercial, No. 75.

Thirteen bottles of beer on the wall,
Thirteen bottles of beer,
If one of those bottles should happen to fall,
There'd be...

irecting a commercial is a specialty. It is not something a movie director does, say, in his spare time. Bob Giraldi has done some work in all aspects of film and television, but he now concentrates almost exclusively on commercials. Besides Lite, he has shot for such varied clients as General Electric, McDonald's, Shasta, Citicorp, Pioneer Hi-Fi, and for Broadway shows such as *Evita*. His favorite commercial of the many he's made is a lovely little vignette about a blind couple that was used to advertise a radio station.

He appreciates that because commercials are not held in the highest artistic regard, he must sometimes suffer peo-ple's condescension for that. But Giraldi is never defensive. When he shot a commercial for the Broadway show *Dream-girls,* the star, Jennifer Holliday, informed Giraldi that she was tired that particular morning and didn't feel like singing.

"Look," he replied. "That's fine. But I just want you to know that approximately eight million people are going to see this commercial. Do you know how many times you have to sell out your theater to reach that number?" He then pauses in telling the story. "She sang," Giraldi says.

He is from Paterson, New Jersey, has lived all his life in and around New York City. "It's all really street," he says, summing up himself and his work. He is handsome, talks very fast, and wears distinctive loose clothes, slipper-type shoes, and pants heavy on the pleats. Giraldi is pleats. "You see," he says, "the stigma is that we're selling a product. Movies are selling tickets, TV is selling ratings, but those directors never have to answer to charges the way I do. But I don't care anymore. Commercials are just right for my pace and energy. Get in, get out. Thirty seconds, a minute. The work reflects my attitude.

"And I like commercials because they're honest. And I like the way takes go rat-a-tat-tat. A lot of people have a tendency to overshoot commercials. Above all, I think people in this business say that there's a believability to my people. I never find my work limiting."

It probably helps with Lite that Giraldi was a pretty fair athlete himself—"competitive," he characterizes it. He must be one of the few rare birds to have attended an art school on a partial athletic scholarship. "I was an artist-slash-jock," Bob says. "I've always understood that middle-class sports mentality." After college he quickly established a reputation for himself as a young director who was good with people, especially with those who weren't professional actors. He directed the commercials that highlighted the personalities on the local Eyewitness News team on the New York ABC affiliate. Included in that group were two ex-jocks, Frank Gifford and Jim Bouton.

"Most athletes do have some sense of theater," Giraldi says. "Even the shy ones. If they're at all comfortable, you can get it out of them." In fact, Giraldi ranks athletes in their own special category among people who appear on commercials: in descending order, actors, performers, athletes, real people. Rarely, he says, has he failed with an athlete. He got nowhere with Lou Brock on a commercial for the Yellow Pages—"He was just too shy to be brought out at all"—and in perhaps another half dozen shootings for Lite he admits that "I could never get the guy to be believable."

On the other hand, Giraldi suffers no illusion that his he-roes are frogs just waiting to be turned into princes under his brilliant tutelage. Few athletes, he believes, ever get to be truly proficient, to embrace real range as actors. Giraldi rates Merlin Olsen as the best actor-athlete he ever saw. "He shows a real sense of drama, genuine emotion," he says. Alex Karras would be his second choice.

Part of Giraldi's own success stems from his confidence. He is never intimidated by the famous names he works with—nor, for that matter, by the size of his minions. Screaming at Boog Powell is nothing unusual for him. Once he took on the whole damn All-Star squad. It was late in the day of the tug-o'-war shoot. Many of the All-Stars had torn their hands on the rope, their energy was low, their faces boiling from a day in the hot sun. "They were mad at everyone, especially me—and rightly so," Giraldi says. But he didn't think they'd found that mystical right "attitude," and he kept on screaming at them.

"You bastards," he hollered, "you sonsofbitches"—and up from there. Still, worse than any names, he then shouted this to them: "Come on, come on. Maybe *your* careers are all over, but mine is just starting."

And they gave him what he wanted. "The guys may look at me and think I'm crazy always stepping on their toes," he says. "But they respect me, I'm sure. I've got a track record for legitimate work, and athletes understand that. You see, they're always at least a little bit afraid that I might be right again."

So now it is the New York Boatyard, ten in the morning, the extras have taken their places around the bar, all garbed in appropriate outdoors attire; Grits Gresham, in his distinctive fisherman's hat, takes a seat, while that veteran lumberjack/ rookie endorser Brian Anderson moves up to stand next to him. They both know the script, but there is a teleprompter running just over the camera. "All right," Giraldi says, "let's try a few practice."

"I once rolled that log off a hundred-foot waterfall, came up standing, and popped myself open a cold Lite Beer from Miller," Brian says, leading off.

"Oh, you lumberjacks," Grits counters. "One time a big-mouth bass pulled me *up* a waterfall. That's why you appreciate Lite Beer. 'Cause it's less filling."

"Yeah, but it was the thought of Lite's great taste that kept me going when I was cutting timber in the great Sahara Forest," Brian replied.

(The original script had read: "Yeah, but it was Lite's great taste that kept me going . . ." but lawyers made them insert the phrase "the thought of." It would be misleading, went the argument, to have anyone suggest that the taste of a beer could actually keep you going. Imagine grown people sitting around and wasting their time over details such as that. But they do. Anyway, time for the big finale.)

"Wait a minute," Grits said. "The Sahara's a desert."

"It is now," Brian said. The extras laughed and guffawed. Giraldi nodded. "Okay, try it again."

They did. When it was over this time, Giraldi told Brian to change "that log" to "a log" in the opening line.

After the third practice take, he told Grits: "Can you slap on your knee without being too hokey? Is that possible?" Grits assured him that was within the realm.

After the fourth practice take, Giraldi, who usually stays quite a ways back where he can watch the action both live and on the monitor that Nick Gisonde watches, stepped forward. "We got to have a point of view," he declared, quite didactically. "When you say less filling, Grits, dammit, say it. The other guys *want* you to argue with them. *Tell* the other guys. Tell them less filling. There should be an attitude. Otherwise, it's just words."

The sixth practice try pleased Giraldi the most. "We're close, very close," he announced. Still, never mind the quali-

ty; it had to be tighter. It was still two seconds over the limit. They had to come in at no more than twenty-seven seconds, leaving three for the product shot and Eddie Barth's voice-over.

Practice number seven Giraldi also fancied. "They're bullshitting more," he said. "You get the feel more, don't you?" Nick nodded. Still, Giraldi had a new idea. He asked someone to get Brian a box to stand on. He checked out that arrangement on the monitor. "No," he decided at last. "He can't stand on that. It'll look like Brian has the longest ankles in the world." Scuttle the box.

But yet another thought. To Nick: "I gotta get Brian to touch Grits' leg." Giraldi stepped up toward the bar again. "Now, Brian, listen to me," he said. "I want you to touch Grits' leg. Now, I know you don't do that up in Connecticut, but believe me, it's okay here. We do that in New York."

Brian laughed and agreed to go along with such urban hijinks.

All during the filming people walked by on Second Avenue, and even though there were all sorts of TV trucks and equipment and people spilling out into the street, almost nobody stopped to look in. They film commercials in Manhattan all the time. It's nothing to go out of your way for.

Grits and Brian tried it again. Giraldi watched the whole scene on the monitor this time. Maybe he was getting ready to shoot. "No," he called out. "*Up* a waterfall! Get it? I want more reaction on up."

Also, Brian was speaking too formally. He had to drop the final *g*s from "cutting" and "standing" and "going." That was going to be his biggest problem all day. "Brian," Giraldi said, "your performance is great. But you've got to talk out. A little bit of bullshitting is permitted in these parts."

They tried a tenth practice run. Same problem. "*Up* a waterfall!" Giraldi cried. "Somebody roll your eyes at *up* a waterfall. Strike an attitude!" But he was pleased enough, and he signaled his assistant to set up. The prop man poured some beer and foamed them with the eggbeater.

"The beers look nice," said the assistant director.

"Yeah, let's go before the beers go down," Giraldi agreed.

"Action!" said the cameraman. "Speed!" said the sound man. "Mark!" said the assistant director. The first take. "Excellent!" Giraldi pronounced it. Still, it was a second too long.

After the next take, Giraldi said: "Brian, give me cutt*in'* timber. No *g*." The cameraman suggested that one of the extras, prominent in red, should be repositioned a bit to the left. They marked a new spot for him.

Third take. Fourth take. "Come on, you're bragging, I know, but make the stories make sense: 'Hey, the Sahara's a desert.' Like that, Grits. Maybe you should say *hey* first. Hey! Don't hesitate. Jump on him."

The fifth take was the best yet, "Very good, just wonderful." But, now for the bad news. "There was no reaction to Brian's first story."

Things plateaued, and by the tenth take Giraldi decided he would rather have more chagrin from Grits when he gets topped at the end. They tried it that way for a couple. "No," Giraldi said. "I like it better when he laughs." Scuttle the chagrin.

On the fifteenth, Giraldi thought maybe the bartender, an actor named E. D. Phillips, should slap Grits on the shoulder. That was a little something extra. "Don't get bored now," Giraldi cautioned the group. "These are great stories you're hearing. They may be the only three stories these guys know, but they're great."

"Good shot," he announced after the next take. "They're all good." It was quarter past eleven now, they'd been at it for well over an hour, and Giraldi called a break. The director pretty much knew now what he could make of this. It wasn't the greatest Lite he'd ever shot, but it was working out well enough. "The scripts are always well written," he said. "They have beautiful nuances. They have the right attitudes. Lite's my strength."

Unfortunately, when the shooting resumed in fifteen minutes something had been lost. Some of the snap had gone out of things. Giraldi grew testier, more sarcastic. "Honey," he called no one male in particular after one desultory take. "Thanks, babe," he sneered after another. And: "All right, girls. Show some one-upsmanship. Exaggerate." Finally things began to get back on the track, and the twenty-fourth take was the best yet. "That was physical. That was everything," Giraldi cried. Unfortunately, the sound man feared that he had picked up a sudden noise from the kitchen.

There was a letdown at that revelation, and the bit soured on the next take. "Grits," Giraldi said, "don't give me oh—oh, you lumberjacks. It's more *ah,* you lumberjacks. And talk with your hands. Demonstrate." Things started improving again.

In fact: for the twenty-eighth take, applause. That could be the one America would see.

For twenty-nine, after all this time, Brian suddenly said "Lite Beer *by* Miller." Cut. Was everybody getting tired? "All right, remember, you've been here awhile," Giraldi said. "You've been at the bar. You're a little tipsy." By the thirty-third take there was applause again. Giraldi was extremely happy. He was sure they had the one they wanted now. Maybe twenty-four, but if not that because of the kitchen noise, then certainly twenty-nine or thirty-three.

"How do you know when you have the one you want?" I asked him.

He thought for a while. "I don't know," he said. "It's more the other way. It's more like you know when you don't have it."

But Nick wasn't that positive. He wanted more takes. "Come on, last one, keep it big," Giraldi said. "One more, that's it, then we'll shoot the product." That meant, give him one more acceptable take, and then they could strike the set and just tape the close-ups of the beer bottles for Eddie Barth to talk over. Still, Nick said he wasn't convinced.

"I know we got it," Giraldi said. Then, to the whole bar, "They can have forty more. It's their money." They had tried thirty-five takes, of which thirty-two had been shot all the way through. It was time to reload a third film cartridge for the camera. It was five minutes past noon.

"Don't get lazy now," Giraldi said. Thirty-six. Thirty-seven. Not bad. Thirty-eight was terrific. "You can't do better than that," he said.

And this time Nick agreed.

"It's a wrap," somebody hollered. Somebody always hollers "It's a wrap" when a commercial is finished.

The Lite Beer commercial No. 75 was done; it would be ready to go on the air in a few weeks. By the time they left the New York Boatyard in another half hour or so, after shooting the product shot, all that was left was to select the best take, tack on the product shot, maybe drop in a little extra sound—some "wild track"—and pick the appropriate Eddie Barth ender, the one that best said: "Lite Beer from Miller. Everything you always wanted in a beer . . . and less" just the right way to round off Grits and Brian.

Be bigger.

MEET YOUR ALL-STARS

RED AUERBACH

Undisputed greatest NBA coach in history . . . Won 11 championships with the Celtics in 13-year stretch . . . Some maintain he is top sports executive in history too, as general manager of Celtics . . . 60th celebrity tapped to make Lite commercial . . . Coached five other All-Stars: Cousy, Heinsohn, the two Joneses, and Nelson . . . Cousy remains only person known who still calls Red by his square name, Arnold . . . Cut Bowie Kuhn from high school team . . . Will retire as Celts' chief executive after 1984 season . . . Although he has worked in the Hub for 30 years, Auerbach has always lived in the nation's capital.

BUCK BUCHANAN

Team captain of 1970 Kansas City Chiefs, Super Bowl champions . . . Played 13 years with K.C., seven straight seasons All-AFL honors . . . One of galaxy of grid stars to come out of Grambling . . . Retired from football in 1976, then coached for Saints and Browns . . . 33rd name to make Lite commercial . . . Currently proprietor of nightclub in Kansas City.

DICK BUTKUS

Linebacker with Bears, made All-NFL all seven of his years in pros . . . Prepped as All-American at Illinois, first on offense as center, then on defense as linebacker . . . Has been announcer for Saints and Buccaneers . . . All-Star since May 1975, 10th commercial aired . . . He was 11th celebrity on air for Lite . . . Working as actor now . . . Many TV, film credits . . . Lives in Los Angeles.

DON CARTER

Only All-Star kegler, voted Greatest Bowler in History in 1970 . . . In 1950s bowled on famous five-man Budweiser (oops) team that has world records still standing . . . Famous for his "bent elbow" style—that's bowling, not Lite drinking . . . Briefly played pro baseball, Class D . . . 38th man to make Lite commercial . . . Calls Miami home now.

BOB COUSY

All-American at Holy Cross, then All-Pro and most famous player in NBA for many years . . . Played on six Celtic championship teams . . . Grew up in Brooklyn, but first language at home was French . . . Coached at Boston College, then for Cincinnati Royals . . . Later became commissioner of American Soccer League . . . 61st on All-Star list . . . Resides in Worcester, Massachusetts, where he is involved in various business ventures and still helps broadcast Celtic games.

BEN DAVIDSON

Late bloomer, was only fourth-round pick in 1961 draft after starring for two University of Washington Rose Bowl teams . . . Left Redskins to join Oakland Raiders in 1953, and there began to carve out reputation as feared defensive end . . . Played three AFL All-Star games . . . Known for deep voice . . . Entered Lite work by doing needlepoint with Rosie Grier and Ray Nitschke . . . 14th man . . . Another All-Star who is a professional actor . . . Appeared in half-dozen movies, more than two dozen TV shows . . . Lives near Oakland, in Pleasanton, California.

FRANK DEFORD

Tabbed 1983 Sportswriter of the Year by vote of National Sportswriters and Sportscasters Association . . . In Sports Illustrated fold since 1962 . . . Also novelist, TV and radio commentator . . . 67th addition to Lite commercial ranks . . . Third All-Star wordsmith, joining Spillane and Gresham . . . Home is Westport, Connecticut.

BOOM-BOOM GEOFFRION

Earned nickname for famous slap shot, which boomed off the boards . . . Nineteen NHL years, 883 games, nine broken noses, one ulcer . . . Best known for Montreal years, anchoring six Stanley Cup champions . . . Coached Atlanta Flames, then, briefly, Montreal Canadiens, before ulcer forced him to leave coaching ranks . . . 16th Lite acquisition . . . Works full time as Miller Brewing rep in Atlanta area, where he has lived for 13 years, now in Marietta, Georgia.

GRITS GRESHAM

Shooting editor for Sports Afield magazine . . . Has written five outdoor books . . . Host on TV outdoor programs, plus long associated with American Sportsman on ABC . . . Hunted and fished all over globe . . . Played briefly in Chicago Cubs' minor-league system . . . Joined Lite as 36th star . . . Past prexy, Outdoor Writers Association of America . . . Home is Natchitoches, Louisiana.

HAPPY HAIRSTON

After starring at New York University, played in NBA with Royals, Pistons, Lakers . . . Best year (18.6 points per game) was same season Lakers set record skein of 33 straight, rolling up 69–13 mark . . . Has been sports broadcaster and acted in several TV shows . . . 46th aboard Lite commercial train . . . Now agent for athletes in Los Angeles area, where he has lived since retiring from the NBA.

TOMMY HEINSOHN

Rookie of the Year for Celtics in 1957 after graduating from Holy Cross . . . Played nine more years, on eight championship teams . . . All-Pro five times with "Tommy Gun" moniker . . . First All-Star to lead a players association, as NBA head (John Mackey led NFL players) . . . 17th Lite addition, first teaming with the late Mendy Rudolph in 1976 . . . Coached Celtics to two titles . . . Insurance agent, landscape artist, broadcaster, actor . . . Resides in Natick, Massachusetts.

JIM HONOCHICK

American League umpire for 25 years . . . Arbiter in seven All-Star games, six World Series, all of which went seven games . . . Temple University graduate, played minor-league ball up to Triple A in Cleveland organization . . . Senior citizen, oldest All-Star, first saw light of day August 19, 1917 . . . 40th on Lite roster . . . Certified not blind . . . Does PR work for First National Bank of Allentown, Pennsylvania, where he has always lived.

DEACON JONES
14 seasons in NFL, with Rams, Chargers, and Redskins, after college career at little South Carolina State . . . All-Pro 10 times, twice named Outstanding Defensive Lineman in league . . . Elected to Pro Football Hall of Fame in 1980, his first year of eligibility . . . Poetry recital made him 22nd name to endorse Lite . . . Has worked as nightclub singer and dancer, and has also appeared in movie and TV dramas . . . Businessman . . . Resides in Inglewood, California.

K. C. JONES
One of the finest defensive guards in basketball history . . . Succeeded Cousy, another All-Star, as Celtic playmaker . . . Not only played with Bill Russell on eight NBA title teams, but also starred with him on two NCAA champion clubs at the University of San Francisco . . . 27th on Lite list . . . After hanging up his black sneakers, coached at Brandeis, then was Laker assistant and led Washington to NBA finals as head coach in 1975 . . . Recently named Celtics head coach, living in Boston.

SAM JONES
Unknown when drafted in 1957 out of North Carolina Central, as last man on first round by Celtics . . . Five-time All-Pro, on 10 championship teams . . . The last of the great bank shots . . . Many insiders pass over West and Robertson and tab Sam the greatest clutch shooter of all . . . 28th star to sign with Lite . . . Coached some after retirement, now works as representative for athletic shoe manufacturer . . . Lives in Wheaton, Maryland, near Washington.

D. D. LEWIS
Last of the "small" linebackers, playing at 215 on 6-foot-1-inch frame . . . Whole career—13 seasons— with Cowboys, after tabbed on sixth round out of Mississippi State in 1968 draft . . . 69th All-Star, made Lite debut with ex-teammate Charlie Waters in fall of 1982 . . . Five Super Bowl appearances ties mark for most . . . Many of best games postseason . . . Double Ds are for Dwight Douglas (Lewis was born just after World War II and named for two generals) . . . Originally from Knoxville, longtime Dallas resident.

JOHN MADDEN
Rang up record 103–32–7 mark as youthful head coach in ten years at helm of Raiders . . . In playoffs eight of 10 seasons, winning 1977 Super Bowl . . . Played briefly with Eagles in 1958 before knee injury wrote finis to play-for-pay career . . . Returned to Cal Poly, where he had been grid and diamond star (tackle and catcher), to earn Master's sheepskin . . . Entered coaching at Hancock Junior College, then defensive coordinator at San Diego State . . . 58th to make Lite commercial . . . Top CBS commentator for the NFL . . . Also radio commentator . . . Fear of flying makes him rail buff . . . Bicoastal, with residences in Pleasanton, California, and New York City.

RODNEY MARSH

"The Clown Prince of Soccer," coaches Carolina Lightnin' of ASL . . . British-born, frequent selection to national team in England, came to colonies in 1976 to star with Tampa Bay Rowdies of NASL . . . Four-time All-Pro . . . Retired 1979, entered Lite campaign next year, 59th name . . . Lives in America now, residing in Matthews, North Carolina, near Charlotte.

BILLY MARTIN

Back in 1983 for third Yankee managerial tour . . . Also skippered Twins, Tigers, Rangers, As, latter in his native Oakland . . . Was "Mr. October" before that name occurred to Reggie Jackson, batting .333 in record-setting World Series play with Bronx Bombers . . . As manager, also led Yanks to three Series, winning in 1977 and 1978 . . . 25th celeb to go to bat for Lite . . . Chairman of the Board of Billy Martin's Western Wear, with stores in New York, Minneapolis, and Clearwater, Florida . . . Resides in Oakland, except on those occasions when George Steinbrenner invites him to manage in The Big Apple.

LEE MEREDITH

Only distaff All-Star . . . Known for her impressive boobs . . . Grew up as Judith Lee Sauls in Passaic, New Jersey . . . Made film debut in The Producers with Zero Mostel . . . Has subsequently appeared on Broadway and in television and films, with more than 100 commercials to her credit . . . Veteran Lite star, first seen in No. 2, July 1973, but wasn't officially tabbed All-Star until 1981, when she became 68th choice . . . House frau . . . Still lives in Jersey, in River Edge.

STEVE MIZERAK

Mixed pool shooting and schoolteaching before Lite catapulted him to fame in 1978 . . . Won U.S. Open four straight years, beginning in 1970 . . . Took World Open in 1976 and many other prestigious titles . . . Early bird, first began playing pool at age four . . . Was youngest member ever enshrined in Billiards Hall of Fame . . . Was 42nd man to star in a Lite commercial . . . Graduate of Athens (Alabama) College . . . Taught social studies . . . Resides in Fords, New Jersey.

DON NELSON

As player, gave proverbial 110 percent . . . Once called by Bill Russell "the quintessential Celtic" . . . On waivers from Los Angeles, passed over by whole NBA, Nelson caught on with Boston, went on to gain five championship rings, play in 465 consecutive games, and score 10,000-plus points . . . 62nd star to join Lite . . . Played collegiately at Iowa . . . Considered officiating career, then started coaching as Milwaukee assistant in 1976 . . . Has been head coach for Bucks since shortly thereafter . . . Blondest male All-Star . . . Lives in Milwaukee.

RAY NITSCHKE

Played 15 years with Packers . . . All-Pro three seasons . . . Most Valuable Player, 1962 championship game, rare honor for defensive player . . . Tabbed top middle linebacker in first 50 years of NFL . . . Was fullback at Illinois, only third-round pro pick . . . You'll usually find Ray with a big cigar in his teeth . . . 14th star to join Lite . . . In Pro Football Hall of Fame . . . Representative for trucking company, he resides near Green Bay in Oneida, Wisconsin.

CARLOS PALOMINO

Held welterweight title for two and a half years . . . Youngest All-Star . . . Compiled lifetime 26–3–3 ring mark before retiring in 1979, then only 29 . . . Born in Tijuana, but has lived in U.S. of A. since he was a six-year-old tyke . . . 55th Lite celebrity . . . Hosts Hispanic TV show . . . Earned college degree at Long Beach State the same year he won world title, only pugilist ever to gain that elusive double . . . Lists Los Angeles as home now.

BOOG POWELL

Capped great Oriole career with MVP designation in 1970 . . . Played in four World Series with Birds . . . Square name is John . . . Finished up with Indian and Dodger sojourns after 14 Baltimore seasons . . . Top home run season was in 1964, with 39 . . . 41st star to make Lite commercial . . . Finished up with 339 major-league home runs . . . Owns and operates the Anglers Marina in Key West, Florida, his home for many years.

FRANK ROBINSON

Only player ever to win MVP award in both major leagues . . . Immediate Hall of Fame choice, 1982 . . . First black manager, with Cleveland, now skippers Giants . . . Played 21 seasons in bigs, starting as Rookie of the Year with Cincinnati, 1956 . . . Fourth on all-time home-run list, with 586 dingers . . . Belted 49 with 1966 Orioles when he led Birds to first World Championship in his first year in AL . . . Entered Lite ranks as 57th star . . . Always considered outstanding team leader . . . Los Angeles is home base.

JIM SHOULDERS

Won a record 16 World Professional Rodeo Cowboys championships, including a never-to-be-exceeded six consecutive all-around titles . . . Was first rodeo star selected for Madison Square Garden Hall of Fame . . . Began his professional tenure in 1942, when only 14 . . . Became 30th Lite TV drinker, and that's no bull . . . Still in rodeo business: owns stock, produces shows, and runs a rodeo school where he lives, in Henryetta, Oklahoma.

BUBBA SMITH

Four times an All-Pro with Colts . . . Was first choice in NFL draft in 1966 after being considered best player in country with Michigan State . . . Brilliant career all but ruined in freak pre-season accident, when he ran into a sideline marker . . . Played in two Super Bowls . . . 29th on Lite roster . . . Just one more All-Star with acting credentials, he is a regular on TV show Open All Night . . . Most recent movie: Stroker Ace, with Burt Reynolds . . . New autobiography entitled Kill Bubba Kill . . .From Beaumont, Texas . . . Brother Tody also played in NFL . . . Now lives in Los Angeles.

MATT SNELL

First All-Star, filmed inaugural commercial in July 1973 . . . Nine seasons with Jets, rushing for a record 162 yards in memorable Super Bowl upset of Colts in 1969 . . . Hails from New York area, but starred for Woody Hayes as Buckeye . . . Has been in several successful business ventures since retiring from the pro grid, most recently as president of Snellco Construction . . . Lives in New York City.

MICKEY SPILLANE

Brooklyn-born, Frank Morrison Spillane, March 9, 1918 . . . Sold millions of books, starting with controversial, I, the Jury, which he dashed off in 19 days in 1946 . . . One of the five most translated writers in world . . . Has played Mike Hammer, his famous private eye, in movies . . . Second All-Star (after Snell), second oldest (after Honochick) . . . Varsity swimmer in college at Fort Hayes, Kansas, then plied trade as natador, working aquacades . . . Boasts trademark crew cut 58 years . . . Lists Murrells Inlet, South Carolina, as home address.

ERNIE STAUTNER

Nine-time All-Pro defensive standout with Steelers after Boston College career . . . Retired in 1964, coached Washington one season, since then with Dallas, where he constructed the Cowboy's famed Doomsday Defense . . . Another veteran All-Star, made the third commercial in 1973 . . . Wins the prize for coming the farthest: born in Bavaria, traditional beer territory . . . Marine during World War II . . . Hall of Fame pick first year eligible . . . Dallas resident.

MARV THRONEBERRY

Better than you think: played in majors over parts of 11 seasons . . . First baseman with power . . . Started with Yankees, traded to Kansas City Athletics in Roger Maris deal . . . Found fame when tabbed Marvelous Marv on 1962 Amazin' Mets . . . Picked up on Lite waivers as 19th man in 1976 . . . Brother Faye also played in majors . . . Retired with 53 major-league home runs . . . Managed insulating company in Memphis before being discovered as beer booster . . . Lives in nearby Colliersville, Tennessee.

BOB UECKER

Good field, no hit . . . Carved out respectable big-league stay with shotgun arm . . . Spent most of career with Braves, but also with Cards, Phillies . . . Moved neatly into broadcasting after retirement, making a new and better career out of denigrating old one . . . Made Lite debut outside bar as the 69th celebrity picked . . . Scores often with Johnny Carson viewers . . . On ABC network sports, and regular Voice of Milwaukee Brewers . . . Knockout after-dinner speaker . . . Lives in Menomee Falls, Wisconsin.

CHARLIE WATERS

Two-time All-Pro with Cowboys, once played in 128 straight NFL games . . . Strong safety, known as coach on the field . . . Began at Clemson as quarterback, finished up on other end of aerials as wide receiver . . . Grew up in North Augusta, South Carolina . . . In 1978 tabbed South Carolina Pro Athlete of the Year . . . Also in Palmetto State Hall of Fame . . . Newest All-Star, entering fold (alphabetically) 70th, after D. D. Lewis . . . CBS color analyst, also is head of Pro-Motion, company that handles engagements and endorsements for celebrities . . . Dallas is home.

BRUCE WILHELM

Only All-Star Olympian, he won a bronze medal as a weight-lifter in 1976 Montreal Games . . . Previously, as a world-class shot-putter, Wilhelm had just missed making the U. S. team in 1972 . . . Mr. Versatile . . . Was also wrestler at Oklahoma State . . . 50th star picked as Lite Beer drinker on TV . . . Won World Strongman title in 1977, retired after defending crown next year . . . Spent several years as high school teacher . . . Now calls San Francisco home.

DICK WILLIAMS

Journeyman gardener for several teams, but heads-up player, now recognized as one of baseball's premier managers . . . Guided Bosox to American League championship in first year at helm, and later won two World Series with Oakland . . . Was 54th Lite choice . . . Also held reins at California and Montreal, now San Diego . . . Resides in Tampa.

THE GREAT LIST

ere, in chronological order, are the first ten years of Lite commercials—every single one aired from July 1973 through June 1983, eighty-one in all.

The commercials are ranked according to their entertainment value, being accorded zero, one, two, or three foamy beers to indicate their quality. Some commercials have also been accorded one or two stars, to signify special historical and/or cultural value.

1. MATT SNELL. Shot in July 1973, at Joe Allen's in Manhattan. Memorable only because it is the first child. Opening line from Snell: "You know, new Lite Beer from Miller is all you ever wanted in a beer . . . and less." Primitive stuff.

2. MICKEY SPILLANE. Shot later that month. Best of the early ones. Gangsters in the background. "What more would a man want on a long, lonely night?" Mickey asks, referring to Lite Beer, as the Doll sashays by in tight-fitting top, swinging a purse. Camera angle features neck-down shot. Lee Meredith is not identified.

3. ERNIE STAUTNER. Rehash of Snell's No. 1, with waitress getting rare female speaking part: "Looks like you're going to take a heap of filling, Ernie." He refers to his friends as "these clowns."

4. BUDDY RICH, Famous Drummer. First commercial shot outside of a bar—in some sort of rehearsal hall. First of only six commercials with any music. Buddy talks jive talk: "The cats in the peanut gallery polished off a few." And maybe he'll "be out of a gig." Dig it. Copacetic. The would-be punch line is something about electric drumsticks. More reach than grasp, but A for Effort.

5. MATT SNELL returns, arm wrestling with JOHN MACKEY, Super Bowl Hero. This was first return engagement first two-man commercial, and first one that didn't refer to friends nelping them drink all the Lites. It also used a bit that would keep popping up with some success: the two stars speaking in unison. Here, they say: "In fact, after I teach this guy a lesson, I'm going to have an-other bottle."

6. SHELDON LEONARD, Famous Movie Tough Guy. Charac-ter actors in this little drama include Large Louie, a gangster, and a moll dressed in red, doing her fingernails. Punch line: "All right, Louie, drop that beer." Not bad acting—for real actors. The first controversial Lite commercial, this one was soon taken off the air for fear that it was "glorifying gangsters." Some viewers had com-plained.

7. MICKEY MANTLE and WHITEY FORD, Baseball Hall of Famers. They speculate about making "the beer drinkers hall of fame." Mantle was better crying for Maypo cereal.

8. JAMES DRURY, Famous Cowboy Star. Don't believe every-thing you read. Another bummer. Outdoors. Three horses make appearances. The gag, such as it is, is that "the bad guys" don't get to drink Lites. Drury chortles. (Say, whatever happened to famous cowboy star James Drury?) But, bad as the commercial was, there was one innovation. For the first time, when there is the product shot at the end, there's an added touch. In this case, a horse whinnies. This sort of gimmick will be used hereafter.

9. DAVE DeBUSSCHERE. Dullsville. Former Knick great chucks a can of Lite into a wastebasket in the locker room. If this keeps up, Gablinger's will have company.

10. DICK BUTKUS. This was shot in May 1975, just as Lite was going national. Whew, just in the nick of time. Hardly the best commercial, but arguably the most important. The tone was set with this one, which was shot in a bowling alley. For the first time an athlete really makes fun of himself. There is also a waitress, a staple of the early commercials. Beer shakes on product shot as if Butkus had bowled down the whole alley. Bob Giraldi debuts as director.

11. RODNEY DANGERFIELD. "I finally found a beer I can re-spect." For the first time, no close-up of a bottle. Camera on Rod-ney all the way to the product shot. A good laugh. Shot in nightclub.

12. ROSIE GRIER and Friends. The buddies are two other large ex-football bruisers, Ben Davidson and Ray Nitschke, but for some reason they are not identified. Neither do they speak. Grier's needlework hobby was well known at the time, and all three are sewing away. This is one of only two commercials ever shot with-out the product-shot ender. The three big guys just hold up the samplers they've been fashioning. Ben's: "Lite Beer from Miller." Rosie's: "Everything you've always wanted in a beer." Ray's: "And less." This commercial was another step toward sophistication, using a well-known personal fact about an athlete to build the story line.

13. MICKEY SPILLANE returns, on a dark street, outside a bar. Intros his hat and trenchcoat this time, too. Very important com-mercial, because it's the first one to address the subject of taste, presaging No. 15. The Doll appears, face and all this time. "What's a nice girl like you doing in a commercial like this?" says Mickey.

14. BOOM-BOOM GEOFFRION. Really just another version of the overworked I'm-not-really-a-tough-guy routine, begun by Butkus, to be extended by Bubba Smith and Billy Martin. In hockey, "you make a lot of enemies . . ." Boom-Boom advises us, and at the end, to prove his point, a whole team of skaters, in full uniform, crash into the bar.

15. TOMMY HEINSOHN and MENDY RUDOLPH. First real classic. "All right, Heinsohn, you're out of the bar." First, and possibly still best of the Less Filling/Tastes Great arguments. Mendy, in referee's uniform, is first Lite official, first sports personality in the commercials not to have been a player.

16. MARV THRONEBERRY. Another good one. McCann-Erickson on a tear; 1976 a vintage year. First outsider mentioned: Carl Furillo. As in: "It takes 43 Marv Throneberry baseball cards to get one Carl Furillo." Probably the only commercial ever filmed in which you hear an announcer on a TV set in the background introducing another commercial: "And now, a word from our sponsor." This was a shocking commercial for Madison Avenue because Marv, the "Baseball Legend," dares suggest bad things for the product, with this tag line: "If I do for Lite what I did for baseball, I'm afraid their sales may go down."

17. WILT CHAMBERLAIN. Like Mantle with cereal, Wilt is better with cars and airplanes, commercial-wise. Still, not bad. This is the one where the bartender is taller than Wilt. "Coming up, Shorty," he says. Wilt wears a leather jacket in this commercial, starting what amounted to a run on that garment then.

18. PAUL HORNUNG. How did this one ever get written? Why did Hornung ever agree to it? Why did Miller allow it? Luckily, everybody came to their senses, and it was yanked after only a cou-

ple of on-air showings. Hornung, walking along a football field, says, "See this face? It's gorgeous." Giddy cheerleaders appear out of nowhere and jump on him. Boo. Hiss.

19. DEACON JONES. In leather jacket, poetry: "Roses are red/Violets are blue/Lite Beer from Miller/I love you." The guys in the bar run away.

20. LE ROY JOLLEY. With his two star horses, Foolish Pleasure and Honest Pleasure. "Am I a trainer or am I a trainer?" Is this a commercial? Barely. And another leather jacket. Shot at the stables. In first 20 commercials, eight were shot away from bars. This will decrease. Jolley is still only person from any kind of racing—horses, cars, or people—to appear in Lite commercial.

21. DICK BUTKUS returns with MIKE ROBERTS, Rugby Star. Least funny of all Butkus star turns. Roberts calls Butkus "Dickie boy" and "Mr. Bootkus." Butkus admires "Those cute little shorts." Forced.

22. BILLY MARTIN. "I feel very strongly both ways. I'm not the kind of guy who gets in an argument"—and a picture hanging on a wall in the background almost falls down. A giggle at the time, but later Martins are all better.

23. NICK BUONICONTI. From the Miami No-Names—remember? "You're . . . ?" "Nick Buoniconti." "No, that's not it." One of the few times an unidentified character actor gets the punch line.

24. K. C. and SAM JONES. "Keeping up with the Joneses." The first of four where the two principals have the same name. K.C. has a leather jacket on. Too obvious.

25. BUBBA SMITH. "I had my own way of tackling. I used to grab the whole backfield. I'd throw the guys out till I found the one with the ball." This line was originally attributed to the late Big Daddy Lipscomb. But then, art imitates life. Punch line: "I also love the easy-opening can." This one was a big hit when it was made, and it improves with age.

26. JIM SHOULDERS. First All-Star to keep his hat on in the bar. Nothing else here: "Giddyap . . . whoa . . . that ain't no bull."

27. GROUP. First Alumni commercial—although it wasn't called that yet. Spillane (with his hat on indoors now) is the leader. "Right, group?" Fifteen other guys and the Doll. First recycling of good old laughs. "I feel strongly both ways. I never argue." "I still don't know why they asked me to do this commercial." "What's a nice guy like you doing in a fight like this?"

28. TOM and DICK VAN ARSDALE. Basketball twins dressed the same, talking in unison. Still, much the best of this genre. "I'm Tom." Or is it: "I'm Dick." "No, you're not. I'm Dick. You're Tom." 2½ foamies

29. BUCK BUCHANAN. "The Buck stops here." Bubba got Big Daddy's line. Buck got Harry Truman's. Commercials make strange bedfellows. Buck is first All-Star to appear in a vest. Mercifully, the leather phase is over.

30. JOE FRAZIER. From a vest to a tuxedo. This was Smokin Joe's show biz era. He sings with a group: "Lite's less filling and that really knocks me out." The ensemble is bopping *out* of a bar—after nine straight commercials shot *in* a bar. Most musical of all Lite commercials. Fun, and well done, too. Surprising they never tried any other All-Star on vocal. Frazier couldn't sing either.

31. BOOM-BOOM GEOFFRION with JACQUES PLANTE. They curse each other in French. *"Sacre bleu!" "Imbécile!"* With subtitles yet! Argument of course, is LF/TG.

32. GRITS GRESHAM. Another All-Star whose shtick is the hat indoors. This is the one where the shade comes down as Grits tells a fish story. First camera trick.

33. RODNEY DANGERFIELD's back and JERRY PARENT, Not-So-Famous Bartender, has got him. Jerry signs an autograph for Rodney. "Would you like mine?" Rodney asks. "Not really," says Jerry. The drum roll that follows really lifts this one near the top echelon. It is also the second time (after Marv) when Miller refers to its own commercials.

34. BATTLE OF THE BIG GUYS. Tug-o'-war on the beach. Second group commercial, with Phil Rizzuto ("Holy cow, look at that!") serving strictly as tug-by-tug announcer, and not as an All-Star—the only time a sports celebrity has been used that way. The Doll, pregnant in real life, replaced by two bikini-clad dollettes, who say, "Hi, Mickey," in unison. Marv sports a hat to protect his bald pate. He finishes with the usual, "I still don't know why . . ." but it still works. Most sophisticated staging so far.

35. DON CARTER. In the bowling alley. He can't open the easy-opening can. Only time trophies are seen in a Lite commercial. Product shot one of the best: 10 Lites aligned like 10 pins.

36. BILLY MARTIN and GEORGE STEINBRENNER. Up close and personal. Most topical Lite commercial—by far—ever filmed. Maybe most topical ever shot by anyone. "Billy, you're fired." "Not again . . ." Steinbrenner is first sports owner to appear (although Dave DeBusschere had become commissioner of the American Basketball Association shortly after he made his early Lite). Also Steinbrenner opens the commercial on the phone—amazingly, the only time a phone is ever used in any Lite commercial.

37. BOOG POWELL and JIM HONOCHICK. Filmed in August 1978, as the campaign completed its fifth year. First bottle close-up in a long time, but of course it's blurred. First All-Stars with eyeglasses since Sheldon Leonard. Honochick is second official to be used, and he gets the good line: "Hey, you're Boog Powell!" One of the best commercials, and the only one to introduce two regulars at the same time.

38. STEVE MIZERAK. "Showing off . . ." First All-Star in a jacket and vest. Record for most takes, but, of course, Steve had to sink a trick shot. Only All-Star permitted to perform sport he is

currently active in for a Lite commercial, which means FCC doesn't consider pool a real sport.
2 foamies
1 Lite insignia

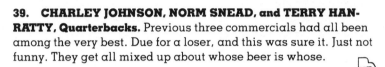

39. CHARLEY JOHNSON, NORM SNEAD, and TERRY HANRATTY, Quarterbacks. Previous three commercials had all been among the very best. Due for a loser, and this was sure it. Just not funny. They get all mixed up about whose beer is whose.

40. HAPPY HAIRSTON. This is the one where the basketball spins by itself in the air. Worst of the special effects. Hairston does a good acting job, but the whole bit is too gimmicky and out of character. In one respect it's in step. It takes place in a bar, as 17 of the last 20 did.

41. POPEYE EGAN, a real-life cop, immortalized by the movie *The French Connection*. But if Popeye was for real, he is the poor man's Mickey Spillane in Lite commercials—right down to his own hat and trenchcoat. "Chasin' bad guys is not so glamorous outside of the movies," Popeye says, and he jabs a beer bottle into a hood's ribs. Three weak ones in a row—first real losing streak in five years.

42. SPEC RICHARDSON and AL ROSEN. It doesn't get any better with these two general managers trading baseball cards. For trivia fans, the outsiders mentioned: Ferris Fain, Bud Harrelson, Gates Brown, Mudcat Grant, Frank Malzone, plus All-Star Boog Powell.

43. TOMMY HEINSOHN. By himself, playing with bottle caps. Not even Heinsohn can save this bummer. What has happened to the Lite Beer ads?

44. MARV THRONEBERRY encores. At last, a passing grade. This one is merely good, though, as Marvelous Marv gets fawned over for being a Lite Beer commercial star. Tag line: "This sure beats baseball."

45. BRUCE WILHELM, Famous Strongman. Once again, the joke is in the reverse: big strong athlete can't even open the beer bottle. Petite waitress comes by and takes the top off. "There you go, Bruce."

46. THE FIRST ANNUAL LITE BEER BANQUET. Best paced of all the group commercials, a top effort by director Giraldi. All your favorite bits in less than a minute. Grits and Mickey in hats. Boom-Boom speaks French. What did he say? "Meat-loaf sandwich and a Lite," explains Mickey. Bubba and Don Carter try the easy-opening cans. Heinsohn and Mendy are seen arguing, although because Mendy died shortly after the commercial was shot, he remains visible only in wide shots. Honochick gets the ender: "Hey, you're Boog Powell." Only it's Bubba, not Boog. A special citation goes to Ben Davidson for best throwaway bit in the whole Lite series, as he puts a flower in Rodney's pocket and says: "Gimme the carrots." You have to see that part.

47. BILLY MARTIN and GEORGE STEINBRENNER. Reprise. This is commercial No. 36 shown over, except when Steinbrenner says, "You're fired," the word "hired" has been dubbed in. Good idea, bad dubbing. Liteologists argue: does this make the commercial No. 36A or No. 47? Answer: No. 47. They counted Grover Cleveland twice, didn't they?

48. DICK BUTKUS and BUBBA SMITH play tennis. First time as a team: Mr. Butkus and Mr. Smith. "We're not just a couple of animals who can only play football." And later, from Bubba: "Tennis anyone?"—a line originally spoken on Broadway by another

tough guy, Humphrey Bogart. Butkus's character is changing, from lead tough to straight man. The product shot is especially cute, showing a tennis racket in an old-fashioned press, with a string broken. Good script, good staging, good all the way.

49. JERRY and MIKE QUARRY. "Saved by the bell." Not really. The Van Arsdales are the only brothers to have when you're having more than one. TKO.

50. WHITEY HERZOG and DICK WILLIAMS. An obvious one: baseball managers giving each other signs at the bar. But this one works better than it reads, because Herzog and Williams come across nicely.

51. CARLOS PALOMINO. "When you come to America, drink Lite Beer . . . but don't drink the water." Good gag, engaging new All-Star, well executed, fun.

52. THE GOLDEN BOY. This means Hornung again—although he is identified only by nickname. At least this one has some charm to it, which his first effort lacked altogether. He gets into a limo, wearing a tuxedo, to join a magnificent pair of long legs. They are not Lee Meredith's. This is the tenth time women have been in a Lite commercial—the Doll four times, all others six. "Practice, practice, practice." Okay.

53. MICKEY SPILLANE. The third time for Mick in a thirty-second. New world record. Lee is back there in the hazy background as he types in his office. "She poured . . . we drank . . . to be continued." Different, but only borderline.

54. BROOKS and FRANK ROBINSON. The only time race is used as a gag. Brooks: "We are not identical twins." Frank: "I'm at

least two inches taller than he is." They used the take in which Frank broke out laughing.

55. THE FIRST LITE BEER ALUMNI PICTURE. The only thirty-second group take, but the largest Alumni crowd of them all: 34 guys, plus the Doll, who does her nails while Rodney tries to take the photograph. Best line is Whitey Ford's: "Knock it off, Billy, you need this job."

56. THE GREAT LITE BEER SHOOTOUT. Sixty seconds, twenty guys, starring Mizerak. The only time Mickey doesn't get the Doll. He just shrugs. Handsome Hornung loses too. "Steve, how do you do that?" "Practice, practice, practice." Deacon's shortest poem: "Quit talking and start chalking." Best characterization of them all.

57. JOHN MADDEN. Anniversary time again: seven years to the month since Matt Snell kicked it off. Madden greets Lite viewers with: "I'm not the same crazy coach who used to storm around the sidelines screaming at the officials," and ends up breaking through the product shot. Watch closely: the bubbles in the real beer stop bubbling only a split second (two frames) before Madden bursts through the paper shot that is substituted. By far the best special effect.

58. RODNEY MARSH. They wanted a commercial with a soccer theme and did the obvious: "Look, Ma, no feet." Marsh is really terrific, though.

59. RED AUERBACH with TOMMY HEINSOHN, K. C. and SAM JONES, plus DON NELSON and BOB COUSY. Nelson local Milwaukee celeb. Red passes the beer pitcher around. "Puhleeze!!"

Red is only All-Star to smoke on camera, his trademark cigar. Cooz and Sam in eyeglasses. By far the biggest group, short of an Alumni shoot, but more isn't necessarily better.

60. PETE STEMKOWSKI. The funniest commercial you never saw. Miller panicked and pulled it off the air almost immediately, because a couple of Polish-Americans whined that it was anti-Polish. Is the Pope anti-Polish? Stemkowski, a hockey player born in Canada, of Polish descent, begins: "You know, with a name like Stemkowski, I've heard a lot of Polish jokes." And then he proceeds to tell a Polish joke, i.e., a joke about Americans, spoken in the Polish language: *"Dalaczego Amerykaminowi zabraklo lodu? Poniewaz zegubil prepis."* The commercial was preshown to various Polish-Americans. They loved it. Liked the joke too (no subtitles): "Why did the American run out of ice? He lost the recipe." Miller ought to stand up for the First Amendment of the Constitution of the United States of America and show this one again.

61. JIM SHOULDERS and BILLY MARTIN. Both in hats. Billy-bawl. "I can tell a real cowboy from the drugstore kind clear across Texas." Mexican music plays, Shoulders goes on: "You see, you don't want to be filled up when you're out there punchin' dogies. Right, cowboy?" Then, the best of the Lite punchlines (by Bob Meury): "I didn't punch that doggie." Hard to beat, unless Lite can work a marshmallow salesman into the act.

62. BILLY KILMER and FRED WILLIAMSON. This is the one where the offensive player and the defensive player argue about their respective units. "The defense rests," the Hammer says. But everybody watching was already asleep by then.

63. THE FIRST ANNUAL LITE BEER BOARD MEETING. The bit here was to decide who was the most popular All-Star. Rodney presiding again. All 22 guys wear boutonnieres. Madden bursts through the chart at the end, but Marv gets the last word: "I knew

this was a bad idea." Lee giggles. Bubba: "Says here the winner is . . ." The only Alumni commercial Giraldi didn't direct; Steve Horn did this one.

64. BOOG POWELL returns with KOICHI NUMAZAWA. It is spring 1981, five years after Mendy and Heinsohn first started the LF/TG argument, but it can still work when the ingredients are right. As they are here. "All right, it's less filling," Boog sighs, as the little Japanese breaks the table with a painful right-hand chop. No subtitles.

65. BUBBA SMITH and DICK BUTKUS, together again. This time on the golf course, with "us linksters" going after fast-moving birdies. "It's a lot easier hitting a quarterback than a little white ball."

66. BILLY MARTIN and MARV THRONEBERRY meet FRANK DEFORD. Far and away the best performance by a sportswriter in a Lite Beer commercial. Billy doesn't speak, only displays method overacting. Marv: "Cheer up, Billy, someday you'll be famous, just like me."

67. RODNEY DANGERFIELD, Famous Swinger. "Hi, you come here often?" Brunette: "Get lost." These are the jokes. That was the best they could come up with: Get lost?

68. THE FIRST LITE BEER BOWLING TOURNAMENT. Of all the Alumni commercials, this one scores the least. You can't teach old jokes new twists. "Deacon's my name, bowling's my game." Honochick bowls the wrong way. Bubba breaks the ball. Madden bursts through. And so on. But, good news for suffragettes: Lee Meredith, who sits as the scorekeeper with Don Carter, is now an official All-Star, first woman to attain this status.

69. CHRISTMAS. Originally shot for the 1981 season, it was shown again for Christmas 1982 as well. Why not every year? It's better than 96.4 percent of all TV Christmas specials. Shot in a den before a roaring fire, it features the All-Star first unit (*sans* Mickey and the Doll), starting off with Butkus, who sets the stage, then Boog, Bubba, Honochick, Grits, Mizerak, Carlos, Martin, Madden, Heinsohn, and Marv, who signs off: "You know, I'm glad they asked me to do this commercial." No product shot, no voiceover. Really lovely.

70. BOB UECKER, Mr. Baseball. Shot outside a bar, this is the twentieth out of seventy not shot inside a bar. Uecker: "Wow, they're having a good time in there." It's not Uecker's fault, but he must work this schmuck shtick in the giant shadow of Marvelous Marv.

71. THE FRIDAY NIGHT LITE BEER CARD GAME, starring Boog (in suspenders), Numa, Jim Shoulders and Mickey (in hats), and the Doll. The best little ensemble in captivity. "Okay, Numa, cut the cards." And this time, the sequel was even better than the original Numa. Shoulders is a sleeper: he gets better with every commercial, but Boog's "oh, no" carries this one right to the top.

72. BEN DAVIDSON. Arm wrestling. Best that can be said for it is that it's a marginal improvement over the Snell-Mackey original arm wrestling, and that Davidson's voice is always worth listening to.

73. BOOM-BOOM GEOFFRION is back. Was he "a pussy cat"? he asks. "If I was a nasty player, may a lightning bolt come down and strike this very spot." Everybody runs out of the bar. The Boom-Boom spots never change very much, but, ironically, he does. He looks younger and slimmer by far than when he first worked a Lite in 1976.

74. TOMMY HEINSOHN and CARLOS PALOMINO. Good odd couple. Mariachis play. Tommy eats the jalapeño pepper and then goes crazy.

75. GRITS GRESHAM matches wits with BRIAN ANDERSON, lumberjack, in suspenders. Tall tales as told by the masters. Introducing to the home screen: the Sahara Forest.

76. CHARLIE WATERS and D. D. LEWIS. You can tell a real cowboy from the Dallas kind clear across Texas. They come back to the stadium to check out the—who else?—Dallas Cowboy Cheerleaders. A short shelf life for this one because feminists complained and Miller winced.

77. SOFTBALL. LFs vs. TGs, one more time. Bowling goes outside. New and improved over last year's. But still too many of the old routines. The Doll is more of an eyeful than ever. "My turn, my turn!"

78. ALFREDO LEAL, bullfighter. That ain't no bull. Generally, foreign sport spots (soccer, rugby) are too obvious. Ouch, again. Anyway: best costume by a Lite actor in a featured role. Two steps ahead of the bull, but barely.

79. BUBBA and BUTKUS, us impresarios. Best continuing series on television. Today the opera, tomorrow the ballet. Big question: where did they find white-tie rentals their size?

80. CORKY CARROLL, surfer. Lite wardrobe department working overtime: the flowered shirt is bitchin', totally awesome. Rare commercial shot away from New York, *cinéma vérité*. Type casting is perfect, too. Surfers are exactly like Corky here. Nice summer viewing.

81. UECKER redux. This sequel far superior to the original. Uecker, posing in bar as Whitey Ford, becomes a likable con man this time, not just a Marvelous Marv clone. Rare case where unidentified actor has large speaking part. Left-handed bit at end worth price of admission all by itself.

Commercials 81—Personalities 74

Shoots failed	5	Horses	5
Shot in bar	59	Twins—Van Arsdales	
Just outside bar	3	Other brothers—Quarrys.	
Other venues	19	Suspenders—Powell, Anderson.	
Deacon poems	5	Tuxedos—Frazier, Hornung.	
Madden breakthroughs	4	Evening clothes—Bubba, Butkus.	
Women: the Doll	11	Writers—Spillane, Gresham, Deford.	
Others	7	Where are they now?—James Drury,	
Music	6	famous cowboy star, Mike Roberts.	
Cigars	Auerbach.	Sixty-second spots 7	
Hats indoors	Spillane,	Announcer—Barth.	
Martin, Shoulders, Grits.		Officials—Rudolph, Honochick.	
		Time—10 years.	

Answers

God is your copilot.
Let your conscience be your guide.
You are not supposed to look here
until you have taken the whole test.

PART ONE

1. *b) six.*
2. *c) Honochick, born August 19, 1917.*
3. *d) Palomino, 33.*
4. *c) The two Pleasures.*
5. *c) Orioles. You probably said Celtics, didn't you?*
6. *b) Chamberlain.*
7. *a) is the only incorrect answer. No habla español.*
8. *d) Parent.*
9. *c) a leather jacket.*
10. *c) timber.*
11. *b) Steve Mizerak.*
12. *d) Dave DeBusschere.*
13. *a) Paul Hornung.*
14. *d) Stautner.*
15. *a) "You know . . ."*
16. *c) Yep, it's breasts.*
17. *c) Shoulders.*
18. *b) Anniversary photograph.*
19. *b) Powell.*
20. *d) Steinbrenner.*
21. *d) golf and f) tennis.*

PART TWO

1. *Dick Williams, Whitey Herzog, Marv Throneberry (cost the Birds $125,000), and Jim Honochick, who played for the Orioles when they were a Triple A team. Did you get it? If you honestly did, give yourself an extra five points.*
2. *No. 35, at the bowling alley with Don Carter.*
3. *When George Steinbrenner rehired Billy Martin, No. 36 was shown again, with Steinbrenner's word "fired" changed to "hired." That became Lite No. 47.*
4. *Holy cow, one of them was Phil Rizzuto, tug-by-tug announcer for No. 34, Battle of the Big Guys. And the other is Koichi Numazawa, a voice of Japanese baseball. Ichi-ban.*
5. *Tommy Heinsohn and Mendy Rudolph.*
6. *Mickey Mantle, Smokin' Joe Frazier, and Nick Buoniconti. Who said he was a No-Name?*
7. *The Christmas Commercial, No. 69, shot late in 1981.*
8. *John Madden coached Ben Davidson on the Oakland Raiders.*
9. *Red Auerbach fired Heinsohn, as coach of the Celtics.*
10. *Frank is two inches taller.*
11. *Bubba Smith. All big guys look alike.*
12. *Pete Stemkowski, in No. 60, asked, in Polish: "Why did the American run out of ice?" Since this commercial was quickly yanked off the air, you probably don't know the an-*

swer to the joke either. Why can't the American read a book and find out for himself?
13. *Only one. Three unnamed horses also appeared in Lite No. 8 with Famous Cowboy Star James Drury.*
14. *Boom-Boom Geoffrion.*
15. *Bubba Smith quotes Big Daddy in No. 25 and Bogie in No. 48.*
16. *Mendy Rudolph.*
17. *Don Carter bowled for the famous St. Louis Budweiser five-man team whose records still stand, twenty-five years later.*
18. *All were mentioned in reference to baseball trading cards. Carl Furillo, Ferris Fain, Bud Harrelson, Gates Brown, Mudcat Grant, Frank Malzone.*
19. *In No. 5, Matt Snell and John Mackey talk in unison as they arm wrestle. In No. 28, Tom and Dick Van Arsdale. In No. 34, the two cupcakes who replaced a pregnant Doll call out "Hi, Mickey" together.*
20. *Mendy Rudolph wore his NBA referee's uniform in the two Lite commercials he made.*
21. *Lite No. 12 is entitled Rosie Grier and Friends. Ray Nitschke and Ben Davidson flank Grier throughout the commercial, doing needlepoint samplers that say, "Lite Beer from Miller" and "And Less" but they never say anything and they are never identified.*

PART THREE

Either answer is correct—for 2 points. If you answered "Both!" you get all 4 points.